W9-ABX-830

SIMÓN BOLÍVAR

Fighting for Latin American Liberation

SIMÓN BOLÍVAR
Fighting for Latin American Liberation

Bárbara C. Cruz

Enslow Publishing
101 W. 23rd Street
Suite 240
New York, NY 10011
USA
enslow.com

Published in 2018 by Enslow Publishing, LLC.
101 W. 23rd Street, Suite 240, New York, NY 10011

Library of Congress Cataloging-in-Publication Data

Names: Cruz, Bárbara, author.
Title: Simón Bolívar : fighting for Latin American liberation / Bárbara C. Cruz.
Description: New York : Enslow Publishing, 2018. | Series: Rebels with a cause | Audience: Grades 7 to 12. | Includes bibliographical references and index.
Identifiers: LCCN 2017003074 | ISBN 9780766089525 (library-bound)
Subjects: LCSH: Bolívar, Simón, 1783-1830—Juvenile literature. | Heads of state—South America—Biography—Juvenile literature. | South America—History—Wars of Independence, 1806-1830—Juvenile literature.
Classification: LCC F2235.3 .C877 2018 | DDC 980/.02092 [B] —dc23
LC record available at https://lccn.loc.gov/2017003074

Printed in the United States of America

To Our Readers: We have done our best to make sure all website addresses in this book were active and appropriate when we went to press. However, the author and the publisher have no control over and assume no liability for the material available on those websites or on any websites they may link to. Any comments or suggestions can be sent by email to customerservice@enslow.com.

CONTENTS

INTRODUCTION

The first Europeans arrived in what is today known as Latin America late in the fifteenth century, beginning with Christopher Columbus's historic voyage in 1492. Looking for gold and silver, the Spanish and Portuguese began exploring the region, mistakenly calling the indigenous peoples "Indians." This contact proved to be devastating to the native population, who had no immunity to European diseases and little defense against European weapons. European explorers such as Hernán Cortés in Mexico and Francisco Pizarro in Peru conquered the native people and began to occupy their lands.

As *conquistadores* (conquerors) began claiming land in the name of the Spanish crown, the *encomienda* system was established. An encomienda was a grant awarded by the Spanish government to colonists settling in the New World. It gave colonists the legal right to force the indigenous peoples to work for them and mandate that they pay for living on their land. The encomienda system led to the extinction of many native groups.

SOUTH AMERICA

Argentina

Bolivia

Brazil

Chile

Colombia

Ecuador

Guyana

Paraguay

Peru

Suriname

Uruguay

Venezuela

Maracaibo •   ★ Caracas   ★ Port of Spain
TRINIDAD AND TOBAGO

VENEZUELA   Georgetown
★ Bogota   **GUYANA**   Paramaribo
COLOMBIA   **SURINAME**

★ Quito
ECUADOR
◉ Guayaquil

Manaus ◉   ◉ Belem   Fortaleza ◉

B R A Z I L

PERU

Lima ★   ◉ Cusco   Salvador ◉

La Paz   ★ Brasilia
★ **BOLIVIA**
Cochabamba ◉   ◉ Santa Cruz

Rio de Janeiro ◉
PARAGUAY   Sao Paulo ◉
★ Asuncion

Porto Alegre ◉

ARGENTINA   **URUGUAY**

Santiago ★
Buenos Aires ★   ★ Montevideo

CHILE

**A modern-day political map
of South America**

Colonizers introduced practices that profoundly changed the region. They brought their religion (Christianity, most notably in the form of Catholicism), their languages (predominantly Spanish and Portuguese in South America), and enslaved Africans to work in the mines and on the plantations established by the Europeans. Eventually over twelve million Africans would be brought to the New World via the transatlantic slave trade, although not all of them survived the difficult voyage. In what was known as "the Middle Passage" (the long trip by sea from Africa to the New World), at least two million Africans died. The economy of Latin America was built on the forced labor of those who survived. Sugar cane, cacao, and indigo production thrived in South America and the Caribbean because of the work of enslaved Africans.

In the New World societies, distinct social classes formed based on race. Segregation was seen throughout society, in education, and in the military. Full citizenship was available to only a small group of elites with European ancestry. Those with African or indigenous backgrounds occupied the lowest rungs on the social ladder.

Spanish colonization of Venezuela began in 1522. By the eighteenth century, the Spanish had established viceroyalties (territories or jurisdictions) throughout the continent. The Viceroyalty of New Granada encompassed modern-day Venezuela, Colombia, Ecuador, and Panama. After almost three hundred years of colonial rule, citizens in the colony began to demand self-governance. They argued that it was unfair for a small European country to dictate how people on a vast continent far away lived.

In Venezuela, the Congress first officially declared the country's independence from Spain and established a republican form of government in 1811. Citizens were allowed to vote for their leaders and the first constitution in Spanish America was written and adopted. Known as the First Republic, it only lasted one year. Economic problems, social inequalities, and a devastating earthquake all led to the fall of the First Republic in 1812.

In 1813, Simón Bolívar launched the Admirable Campaign, restoring independence to Venezuela and establishing the Second Republic. But this government would also be short lived. Under the military direction of José Tomás Boves, the Spanish army defeated Bolívar and his forces, the *independistas*, in 1815.

Bolívar retreated to safety in Haiti, simultaneously securing financial and military support from Haitian president Alexandre Pétion. Bolívar then entered Venezuela in 1817, setting up his military headquarters in the Orinoco River Valley. After two years of brutal fighting, Bolívar's forces defeated the Spanish and a new constitution was created. Elected the president of the Third Republic of Venezuela, Bolívar had hopes that the whole of South America could be united as a free and independent coalition of republics. Although he fought hard to make this dream a reality, he would be unable to realize all of his goals for South America. But his vision and efforts earned him the name El Libertador ("The Liberator"), assuring that he would never be forgotten in history.

1

Love and Loss

Fifteen-year-old Simón Bolívar was excited about his trip to the Old World. It was January 1799, and although he loved Venezuela, his country of birth, he was looking forward to visiting his family's ancestral home, Spain. With letters of introduction from government officials in hand, Bolívar set sail on the *San Ildefonso*, a Spanish warship. At the time, the British had set up blockades against the Spanish in the Caribbean. The *San Ildefonso* was a lighter craft, designed to travel quickly and evade enemies. The ship first stopped in Veracruz, Mexico, to pick up cargo. But an English blockade prevented the ship from sailing and the *San Ildefonso* spent seven weeks in port. Bolívar took advantage of the delay and traveled inland to visit Mexico City. With a letter of introduction he had been given in Venezuela, Bolívar was able to meet the viceroy, the regional ruler appointed by the Spanish monarch, in the capital. At their meeting, the young man expressed his admiration for the revolutions that had recently occurred in France and North America, much to the surprise of the viceroy, who represented colonial rule.

The ship set sail once again and made a brief stop in Havana, Cuba. There the ship picked up food and water for the long voyage to Europe. Chickens, goats, sheep, and

Simón Bolívar was known as El Libertador for his role in liberating South American colonies from colonial rule.

cattle were brought on board. When they finally arrived in Spain in May 1799, the ship, sailors, and passengers were tired, hungry, and dirty. After so many weeks at sea, it must have been a relief for Bolívar to set foot on solid land.

Bolívar's uncle, Esteban Palacios, was living in Madrid and would be instrumental in introducing him to important citizens in the Spanish capital. One of these aristocratic citizens was the nobleman Marqués Gerónimo de Ustáriz, who opened his home to the young Bolívar and soon became his guardian and mentor. Ustáriz was a fellow Venezuelan who had moved to Spain and had progressed through the government ranks; he was now minister of the war council, an important position. Bolívar

MARQUÉS GERÓNIMO DE USTÁRIZ

Like Simón Bolívar, Gerónimo de Ustáriz was originally from Caracas, Venezuela. Born in 1735, Ustáriz was the son of a prominent economist, Luis Gerónimo de Ustáriz y Gandía, who had arrived in Venezuela in 1730. The aristocratic family lived a life of privilege in Caracas. The young Gerónimo received the best education available at the time. He also inherited the title of "marquis" from his uncle, Casimiro de Uztáriz who first held the title. This title of European nobility ranks just above a count.

Some historians consider Ustáriz to be Bolívar's most important teacher. Ustáriz reintroduced him to writers Bolívar had studied while he had been a student in Venezuela, but now with a more studious focus. As evidence, these historians point to letters written by Bolívar, comparing those he wrote before his trip to Europe with those he composed after he had lived with Ustáriz for a year. His writing became clearer, more elegant, and more intellectual.

As his legal guardian and mentor, Bolívar asked Ustáriz for his support when he proposed marriage to María Teresa Rodríguez del Toro y Alaiza. Ustáriz consented to the wedding but agreed with María Teresa's father that it should be postponed until the youths were a bit older. Ustáriz was instrumental in organizing the ceremony and was in attendance to see his young apprentice marry.

After marrying and leaving Europe, Bolívar kept in touch with Ustáriz. But the marquis did not have many more years to live. In 1809, Ustáriz died at the age of seventy-four.

moved to the marquis's house in early 1800, and Ustáriz became his legal guardian.

In Ustáriz's well-stocked library, Bolívar embarked on a course of study, voraciously reading books in history, philosophy, languages, and more. Bolívar enrolled in fencing, riding horses, and dance lessons and purchased the latest fashionable clothing. An intelligent conversationalist, Bolívar sharpened his social skills by listening and participating in the marquis's social gatherings. He was exposed to the most educated and refined citizens of European society. It was at one of these get-togethers that Bolívar met María Teresa Rodríguez del Toro y Alaiza.

María Teresa was the only daughter of a Spanish mother and Venezuelan father. She was quiet, intelligent, and sweet-tempered, with coffee-colored eyes and a pale complexion. Her "shy and gentle nature" was said to have captivated Bolívar.[1] He was enchanted and soon asked to be her *novio* (fiancé). Although María Teresa was two years older, her parents acknowledged that Simón was well-positioned to take a bride, given the many thriving businesses and properties he had back home in Venezuela. However, because of his youth, the couple would need to postpone the marriage by a year or two.

A park sculpture of María Teresa and Simón in Spain

Simón and María Teresa were married on May 26, 1802, in a Catholic ceremony in Spain. The groom was anxious to show his bride her new home in Venezuela. On June 15, they set sail for Venezuela and they arrived

MARÍA TERESA RODRÍGUEZ DEL TORO Y ALAIZA

María Teresa was born in Madrid, Spain, in 1781. Her father, Bernardo Rodríguez del Toro, had been born in Caracas, Venezuela, to an aristocratic family. María Teresa's mother, Benita de Alaiza Medrano, was from Valladolid, Spain. Benita died while María Teresa was still young and so she was raised by her widower father.

Simón met María Teresa in 1800 at the home of the Marqués Gerónimo de Ustáriz. Some historians describe that she was not a great beauty, but that Bolívar was taken by her gentle personality and natural intelligence. Others say that her dark hair and lively eyes charmed Bolívar. But by all accounts, Bolívar was immediately smitten by her. He compared her to a precious gem and treasured her for the rest of her life.

Although Simón Bolívar had other loves during his life, María Teresa was the only wife he ever had.

in Caracas on July 12. Among the various homes and haciendas (large estates) the young couple could settle in, Bolívar chose the hacienda in San Mateo, his family's ancestral home in Venezuela and the center of the family fortune. The San Mateo property had been in the family for two hundred years.

The young couple enjoyed being newlyweds and establishing a home together. While Simón supervised the operations at the hacienda, María Teresa settled into her new life as wife and grand dame of the estate. They spent several happy months together, enjoying their new marriage.

Simón and María Teresa's wedding was held in Spain in 1802.

But then tragedy struck, shattering the young couple's happiness. María Teresa came down with a high fever—probably either malaria or yellow fever—and became very ill. As Simón helplessly watched his young bride's condition worsen, he became despondent. Sadly, on January 22, 1803, María Teresa died, leaving Simón in deep grief. They had only been married eight months.

María Teresa del Toro y Alaiza was buried in the Cathedral in Caracas, where Simón's parents were also buried. Simón declared he would never remarry, a vow he would keep for the rest of his life.

> **"I loved my wife dearly, and her death caused me to vow that I would never marry again; I have kept my word...had I not been widowed perhaps my life would have been different."[2]**

In his grief, Bolívar decided it would be best to leave Venezuela and return to Europe. Little did he know that his start in politics was just beginning and he would one day be known as the Liberator.

2
A Venezuelan Childhood

S imón Bolívar was born on July 24, 1783, in Caracas, Venezuela. He was baptized with his full name, Simón José Antonio de la Santísima Trinidad Bolívar y Palacios. Simón was the fourth and youngest child in the family. He had two sisters, María Antonia and

Simón's birthplace and home in Caracas is now a museum.

Juana Maria, and a brother, Juan Vicente. The family had one more child, a daughter named María del Carmen, who died at birth.

The Bolívar family lived in a large, well-furnished house near the city's main square. The Spanish colonial building was one story and held rich furnishings and draperies. As was fashionable at the time, the house had two courtyards with lush green plants and a fountain. During warm weather, the courtyards offered welcome relief from hot temperatures.

Simón's father, Colonel Juan Vicente Bolívar y Ponte, had been born in 1726 to one of the wealthiest families in Venezuela. His family owned cocoa and sugar plantations and sold fine fabrics to well-to-do Caraqueños (citizens of Caracas). At the young age of twenty, he was elected the general attorney for the city. He had a long and storied career in the military and at times expressed anticolonial

A cathedral in Caracas built in the Spanish colonial style

sentiments. In a letter written in 1782, Simón's father complained about Spanish rule: "We find ourselves in a shameful prison…We have no choice but to throw off this unbearable and disgraceful yoke."

Simón's mother, María de la Concepción Palacios y Blanco, came from a landholding family of government officials. Her family's ancestors included some of the original founders of Caracas. Juan Vicente and María de la Concepción were married in 1773—he was forty-six years old, she was not quite fifteen.

The Bolívar family were well-to-do criollos (Creoles) who had migrated from Spain two hundred years before, when the European country had started claiming land in the New World. Spain began colonizing Venezuela in 1522 and founded Caracas in 1567. The city, located in a mountain valley in the north, grew and prospered. It was close to the sea, had public gardens and plazas, and beautiful churches built in the Spanish colonial style. A European visitor commented on the city, observing: "The city of Caracas revealed itself to us with sufficient majesty …it appeared large, clean, elegant, and well built."[2]

The Bolívar family owned the house in Caracas where Simón was born as well as sugar cane, indigo, and cacao plantations; silver, gold, and copper mines; and cattle ranches in the surrounding areas. Of particular importance was the sugar cane plantation in San Mateo, which had been the center of the family's fortune since they first arrived in New Spain. To manage and work all of these properties, the family owned thousands of slaves.

The Bolívar family was part of the elite society in Venezuela known as *mantuanos*. Mantuanos were wealthy citizens who owned multiple properties, businesses, and slaves. They got their name from the *mantos*, or capes, that the women wore. A lady of the mantuano class often made a big show of how many assistants she employed to go to mass at church—one to carry her prayer book, another to carry her personal items, and yet another to spread a piece of carpet before her.

After Simón was born, his mother's health prevented her from nursing the newborn. The baby's life was in danger without mother's milk. As was the practice among many elite families at the time, a slave was found to serve as a "wet nurse" for the baby Simón. Wet nurses breastfed and cared for children who were not their own. The newborn Simón was given to a young slave named Hipólita at the San Mateo estate to care for him. Simón developed great affection for Hipólita, later saying "I know no other parent but her."[3]

When Simón was not quite three years old, his father Juan Vicente, became gravely ill. In his will, he left his properties to his wife and children. On January 19, 1786, Juan Vicente died, leaving his family in mourning. His widow got down to the business of raising her children and managing the family's properties and industries.

Tragedy was to strike again as Simón neared his ninth birthday. His mother contracted tuberculosis, a deadly bacterial infection that attacks the lungs. At the time, there was no known cure for the disease. After a three-month illness, Simón's mother died. After María de la Concepción's death in 1792, her father moved his grandchildren and Hipólita into his home. But soon after, the children's grandfather also became ill and passed away just a year later in 1793.

Following the death of their grandfather, the two Bolívar sisters (aged thirteen and fourteen) married and went to live with their husbands. Simón and his brother

This statue of Hipólita is in a park in Valencia, in the State of Carabobo, Venezuela.

went to live with two different bachelor uncles. Simón was sent to live with his uncle Carlos, with whom he would often clash. Separated from his brother and sisters, the orphaned boy was often lonely.

Bolívar spent much of his free time on his own, with other youngsters in town. He was in contact with people from all of the social classes, including those who were very poor and of different ethnic backgrounds. He spent time with *mestizos, mulatos, pardos*, and those in his own class, the mantuanos. When children were born, the shade of their skin was noted on official documents. Later, people were even taxed according to the color of their skin. The largest percentage of the Venezuelan population were the pardos; despite their numbers, they often felt excluded from society because of their mixed ancestry. This interaction likely impacted Bolívar's thinking about racial discrimination and would later be evident when he became a political leader.

CLASSES OF SOCIETY IN COLONIAL VENEZUELA

Society in colonial Venezuela was very much divided. Your family's status when you were born could dictate the path that your life would take. Not only was social class linked with one's economic status, but it was also linked with one's race. Those who had "pure" European ancestry often would rank the highest in this social system, while those with African or indigenous ancestry would often be relegated to the lower social classes. Social classes in Venezuela included the following:

A *criollo* was a white person of Spanish descent born in the New World.

An *esclavo* was an African slave.

A *mantuano* was someone who belonged to the Venezuelan aristocracy.

A *mestizo* was someone of mixed ancestry, typically indigenous and European.

A *mulato* was someone of both African and European ancestry.

A *pardo* was a free person with some African ancestry.

A *peninsulare* was someone who was born in Spain and was now living in the New World.

A *zambo* was a person of mixed indigenous and African ancestry.

Although some accounts say that the young Bolívar was not a serious student, he nonetheless learned mathematics, history, politics, and languages, like most boys of his age and social station. The well-known German scientist Alexander von Humboldt—whom Bolívar would meet many years later—found the Caraqueños whom he visited to be well-educated and intellectually curious. He wrote: "I have found among the families of Caracas a decided taste for learning, a knowledge of the important

German scientist Alexander von Humboldt studied the plants and animals of South America.

27

works of French and Italian literature, and a notable predilection for music which they cultivate successfully and which, like all fine art, serves as a nucleus, attracting the various classes of society."[4]

"We are not Europeans; we are not Indians; we are but a mixed species of aborigines and Spaniards. Americans by birth and Europeans by law."[5]

Bolívar liked to read and he read many of the works of Enlightenment thinkers. The Enlightenment was an intellectual movement that advanced ideas such as liberty, reason, and the separation of church and state. Over the years, Bolívar had four teachers: Andrés Bello, Father Andújar, Guillermo Pelgrón, and Simón Rodriguez. Although he received lessons from all of them, it was Rodríguez with whom he would form a lifelong teacher-student bond.

Don Simón Rodríguez often delivered his lessons to the young pupil underneath a great tree in the family's backyard. Don Rodríguez also taught him how to swim, ride horses, and conduct himself in "polite" society. When a clash with his guardian uncle prompted Bolívar to run away, the family sent the boy to live with his tutor. The boy argued: "If slaves have the freedom to choose their masters according to their own satisfaction, I should at least not be denied the freedom to live where I please."[6] During the two months that Bolívar would live with Rodríguez, their friendship deepened—a friendship that would last all their lives. Later Simón would remember his tutor as someone with "grace and talent...a teacher who instructs in an amusing fashion."[7]

THE ENLIGHTENMENT

The Enlightenment was a philosophical and intellectual movement that developed in the late seventeenth century with the beginning of the Scientific Revolution. It placed science and reason above traditional ideas and practices. Enlightenment thinkers wrote about concepts such as equality, liberty, and the separation of church and state. These ideas influenced the thinking of people in Europe, the Caribbean, and North America, leading to the French, Haitian, and American Revolutions.

Notable Enlightenment writers include René Descartes, John Locke, Thomas Hobbes, and Jean-Jacques Rousseau. Descartes, a mathematician, applied reason to the solving of complex mathematical problems. Locke argued that all men are by nature free and equal to each other. Further, he said that people have the right to replace governments that stop protecting and working for them. Hobbes advanced the importance of physical laws and how they resulted in cause and effect relationships. Rousseau's social contract theory claimed that by joining together and agreeing to work collectively for the good of society, people could create a just civilization.

Enlightenment thought profoundly impacted Bolívar, who often reflected on his studies and quoted them in his quest for Latin American independence.

When Bolívar was fourteen, Don Simón Rodríguez was accused of being involved in a conspiracy against the Spanish government in Caracas. Although no evidence was found against him, Rodríguez left the country quickly, under threat of hanging. Although Bolívar was sad to see his tutor go, they would meet up again soon on another continent.

With his beloved tutor gone, Bolívar was registered in a military academy originally established by his father, the Milicias de Aragua. As a cadet (military student) there, he learned about military history and strategy tactics. He completed his studies with a good, though unremarkable, academic record. Very soon Bolívar would be putting these lessons to good use.

3

Travels in Europe

Bolívar's first visit to the Old World had been in 1799 when he was sent to continue his studies. During that time he not only deepened his knowledge of traditional school subjects, but he also met and married María Teresa Rodríguez del Toro y Alaiza. The couple moved to Venezuela shortly after the wedding and spent a few months of newlywed happiness at the Bolívar family plantation in San Mateo. Sadly, their happiness did not last; María Teresa died just a few months after arriving in Venezuela.

After spending an unhappy and difficult year in Venezuela as a young widower, Bolívar decided to return to Europe. Many years later, Bolívar said:

> *"I loved my wife dearly, and her death caused me to vow that I would never marry again; I have kept my word...had I not been widowed perhaps my life would have been different...when I arrived in Caracas from Europe with my bride in 1802, let me say at once that my mind was filled only with the emotions of passionate love and not with political ideas, for these had not yet taken hold of my imagination."*

Bolívar met the German scientist Alexander von Humboldt when he was visiting France in 1804.

But this would all change with the life-transforming trip he would now embark on.

In late 1803, Bolívar set sail for Europe once again, arriving in Spain in time for New Year's. He first visited his wife's family and they mourned her death together. He later remembered: "Never shall I forget my meeting with Don Bernardo [María Teresa's father] when I gave him the mementos from María Teresa. Son and father mingled their tears. It was a scene of sweet sorrow—or the sorrows of love are sweet."[2]

But Spain did not hold Bolívar's attention for long. Soon he decided he would instead live in Paris, France, and visit other European countries while living there. Bolívar thrived in Paris, attending cultural events, meeting new people, and spending money on luxury goods and gambling. He also continued his education, reading a wide range of authors and works in philosophy, history, and poetry. His favorite author, Voltaire, wrote forcefully about the separation of church and state and people's rights to freedom of speech and religion. Bolívar also read the works of other Enlightenment thinkers such as John Locke, Thomas Hobbes, and Jean-Jacques Rousseau. Enlightenment philosophy influenced people in Europe, the Caribbean, and North America, leading to the French, Haitian, and American Revolutions. Each of the writers Bolívar studied left an imprint on his thinking about Latin America's quest for independence from colonial rule.

While in France, Bolívar met the German naturalist and scientist Alexander von Humboldt. Humboldt had spent the preceding five years traveling throughout the Spanish colonies in the Americas, publishing his findings

The emperor of France, Napoleon Bonaparte, in 1804

about the geography, plants, and animals he saw there. He also wrote about his impressions of societies he visited in Latin America. About Caracas, Venezuela, he glowingly wrote: "In no other part of America has society taken on a more European character…One feels nearer to Cádiz [Spain] and the United States than in any part of the New World."[3] Bolívar shared his dream of his country's independence from Spain with Humboldt, but the naturalist replied: "I believe that your country is ready for its independence. But I cannot see the man who is to achieve it."[4] Later, Bolívar would closely study von Humboldt's detailed maps and descriptions of his travels as he made his military plans.

During Bolívar's stay in France, one of the experiences that most impressed him was witnessing the coronation of Napoleon Bonaparte in Paris's Notre Dame Cathedral. The coronation ceremony was a luxurious affair that cost the government millions of francs, the French currency. Surrounding streets had been paved and nearby houses were destroyed to make room for the event. It was different from past coronations in that the sitting pope, Pope Pius VII, presided over the event. Bolívar was captivated by the coronation and the devoted following that Napoleon enjoyed. Years later he said,

"I saw the coronation of Napoleon in Paris. The magnificent ceremony filled me with enthusiasm, less for its pomp than because of the sentiments of love which an immense crowd showed for the French hero…What seemed great to me was the universal acclamation and the interest which his presence inspired."[5]

35

NAPOLEON BONAPARTE AND LATIN AMERICAN INDEPENDENCE

Napoleon Bonaparte's fame and reputation grew during the French Revolution (1789–1799). As a military leader, he is considered to be a brilliant strategist, having won most of the battles he fought in. He became emperor of France in 1804 and ruled for the next ten years.

In 1808, Bonaparte dethroned the Spanish king, Ferdinand VII, and replaced him with his brother Joseph Bonaparte. As new governments were set up in Spanish America, loyalties were divided in the region. Some citizens remained faithful to Ferdinand, some accepted the new French leadership, and yet others became convinced that independence from Europe was the only appropriate course of action. Many historians consider Napoleon's actions an underlying cause of the wars for independence in Latin America. Although Ferdinand VII was reinstalled as monarch of Spain in 1814, the seeds of revolution had already been planted.

In April 1814, Napoleon was forced to abdicate his rule and a new king of France, Louis XVIII, was installed. Napoleon was exiled to the island of Elba, off the coast of Italy. Less than one year later,

Napoleon escaped Elba and returned to France, determined to recover his power. For the next three months, referred to as the Hundred Days, Napoleon tried to reclaim his control of France. His forces were eventually defeated in the Battle of Waterloo on June 18, 1815. He was again forced to abdicate and this time was exiled to the island of Saint Helena off the west coast of Africa. Living conditions were difficult on the remote island and Napoleon died there in 1821.

But Bolívar also criticized the new emperor, believing that Napoleon was betraying the principles of the French Revolution for his own gain. Like many of his contemporaries, Bolívar believed in revolutionary ideals and supported the overthrow of monarchies to be replaced with democratic republics. Bolívar said: "The crown which Napoleon placed on his head I regarded as a miserable thing."[6] While Napoleon instituted some of the revolutionary changes, he soon became a dictator and built a large empire across much of Europe. Bolívar later said of the coronation, "From that day, I regarded [Napoleon] as a hypocritical tyrant."[7]

> **"Flee the country where a lone man holds all power: It is a nation of slaves."[8]**

While in France, Bolívar was delighted to find that his old tutor, Simón Rodríguez, was living there too. Rodríguez and Bolívar resumed their philosophical discussions. Bolívar's former teacher was deeply influenced by philosopher Jean-Jacques Rousseau's

The Social Contract. In it, Rousseau argues that legitimate political authority can only come from the people, not monarchs. Rodríguez shared Rousseau's philosophy with his student who would later quote and praise Rousseau in letters and journal entries. Bolívar credited Rodríguez with his intellectual formation, saying to his tutor: "You formed my heart for liberty, for justice, for the great, for the beautiful …You cannot imagine how deeply engraved upon my heart are the lessons you gave me."[9] Many historians believe that it is during this time period that Bolívar began to seriously question the authority and legitimacy of the Spanish crown in the Americas.

Along with their friend Fernando Toro, Bolívar and Rodríguez decided to embark on a trip from France to Italy in 1805. Much of the trip was done on foot, including crossing the Alps into Milan, Venice, and Florence. Their trip ended in Rome, where they were captivated by the ruins of the ancient city. As part of his education, Bolívar had read the writings of the ancient Greeks and Romans. The tutor and the student visited the Monte Sacro (Sacred Mount) hill in Rome. In ancient Rome, Monte Sacro is where Sicinius, a leader

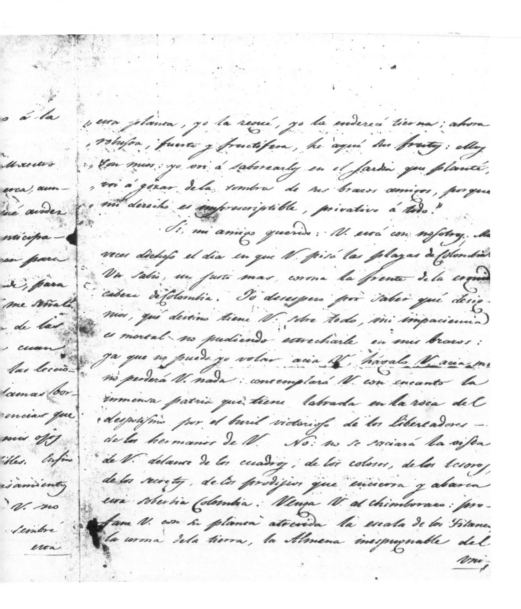

Bolívar wrote this 1824 letter to his tutor, Simón Rodríguez.

of the plebeians, or the lower classes, led a revolt against the patricians, or the upper classes. The plebeians set up a camp on the Monte Sacro and threatened to secede from Rome. The patricians eventually agreed to increased rights for the plebeians, including having their own elected officials.

Under the watchful eye of his tutor, Bolívar took this oath on Monte Sacro, vowing to liberate the Americas from the Spanish crown: "I swear before you; I swear by the God of my fathers; I swear by my fathers; I swear on my honor; and I swear by my country that I will not rest body or soul until I have broken the chains with which Spanish power oppresses us."[10] Like the vow he took about never remarrying, Bolívar would take this vow seriously and would pledge his life to the Latin American independence movement.

Another curious event happened while Bolívar was in Rome. The Spanish ambassador to Italy invited Bolívar to accompany him to the Vatican. The Vatican is where the Catholic Church is centered. The pope, who leads the Catholic Church, lives there. The Spanish ambassador and Bolívar had an audience with Pope Pius VII, the pope at the time. It was customary to kneel and kiss the cross of the pope's shoe, but the nonreligious Bolívar refused. The Spanish ambassador was embarrassed, but the pope did not take offense, saying: "Let the young man from the Indies do as he pleases."[11]

After Bolívar returned to Paris, he told friends that he had been thinking of the future of Spanish American and planned to return to Venezuela. In 1806, Bolívar decided it was time to return to his homeland. Traveling with him was his nephew Anacleto, who would start attending school in Philadelphia, in the new nation of the United States. Bolívar escorted his nephew to the United States, getting the chance to see the new democracy at work in the recently established country. He visited the cities of Charleston, South Carolina; Washington, DC; New York City; Boston, Massachusetts; and ended in Philadelphia, Pennsylvania. Later, Bolívar reflected, "During my brief visit to the United States I saw rational liberty for the first time in my life."[2]

BOLÍVAR'S TRIP TO THE UNITED STATES

Although no written documents exist of Bolívar's approximately five-month visit in the United States, historians can piece together his impressions from his later correspondence and from historical records of the day.

When Bolívar visited the United States on his way home to Venezuela, Thomas Jefferson was president of the young country. Just three years before, President Jefferson had asked Congress for funding for the Lewis and Clark Expedition. Led by Meriwether Lewis and William Clark, the team of about forty-five men set off from the east to explore the continent's northwest region. When they returned in 1806, they shared with the American

(continued on the next page)

(continued from the previous page)

people information they had collected about the geography of the land, the plants and animals they encountered, and the native people who lived there. It was a time of growth, discovery, and possibility. Bolívar would have learned about this historic trip as he visited the United States

When he visited Washington, DC, Bolívar was also deeply influenced by a chance encounter with President Jefferson. One day he saw the simply dressed, unescorted president riding his horse to his office. It impressed Bolívar that the leader of a great, new country could be humble in his governance and still command the respect of the people.

Bolívar left the United States with a generally positive impression of the recently formed nation. He made note of the aspects of democracy (such as education for all) he believed could be applied to Spanish America, as well as those (such as slavery) to which he was opposed. Although he would remember the lessons he learned in the United States, his visit would be the first and only time Bolívar would set foot in North America.

Now that he was on his way back to Venezuela, what would Bolívar find when he arrived? Would the criollos listen to his ideas? Were the people ready to revolt against the Spanish crown? And who would lead the people to independence? These may have been questions on Bolívar's mind as he journeyed back home.

4

Independence for Venezuela

W hen Bolívar returned to Venezuela in 1807 after his time in Europe, he found his homeland in crisis. In addition to colonial rule, many areas were ruled by *caudillos*, regional military or political leaders that divided people's loyalties. Caudillos ruled individual regions, with each region pledging their alliance to the caudillo. People often trusted a local caudillo more than they did a political leader at the national level. This situation prevented a cohesive, organized uprising throughout the country. To gather all the distinct groups, a leader would need to emerge with an inclusive vision.

Francisco de Miranda, a military leader, had been leading a revolution against the Spanish crown. Miranda had participated in the American Revolution in the attack on Fort George against the British in Pensacola, Florida, in 1781. Ten years later, Miranda also served in the French Revolutionary Army, earning the rank of general. In 1792, while visiting London, he met the Peruvian Jesuit priest Juan Pablo Vizcardo y Guzmán, who was living there in exile. Vizcardo had written an essay, "Letter to Spanish Americans," in which he urged Latin American colonists to demand their rights from the Spanish crown. In the opening paragraph, he wrote: "The New World is our

Venezuelan general Francisco de Miranda paved the way for Simón Bolívar.

country; its history is ours." Miranda translated the essay for publication, in support of Vizcardo's beliefs.

These experiences convinced Miranda that it was time for his native Venezuela to become independent, too. Like Bolívar, he had been born in Caracas, but was born thirty-three years before Bolívar. When Bolívar learned of Miranda's plan, he wrote him a letter saying, "At the first sign from you, we are ready to follow you as our leader to the very end, and to shed the last drop of our blood in this great and honorable undertaking."[2]

FRANCISCO DE MIRANDA

Although Simón Bolívar is called the Liberator, Francisco de Miranda is considered in many Latin American countries to be Bolívar's predecessor. Miranda, many would argue, paved the way for Bolívar.

Born in 1750 in Caracas, Venezuela, Miranda attended the best schools available. He was a good student and, in 1767, at the age of seventeen, he graduated from college. A few years later, Miranda traveled to Madrid, Spain, where he continued his education by avidly reading, building a personal library that would continue to grow over his lifetime.

Miranda fought for Spain as a young soldier and then participated in the American Revolution, the French Revolution, and in the Latin American wars

(continued on the next page)

(continued from the previous page)

for independence. In 1804 Miranda began to devise a military plan to liberate Venezuela from Spanish rule. Although it was to be short-lived, Miranda was instrumental in establishing the First Republic of Venezuela.

Miranda did not live long enough to see the liberation of his country—or others in Latin America. But for his vision, he is called "El Precursor" (The Precursor) in many Latin American countries, acknowledging his important efforts in the independence movement.

Miranda went to the United States to prepare the *Leander*, a brigantine ship, and two smaller schooners, *Bacchus* and *Bee*, with military equipment. He also recruited soldiers, purchased arms, and acquired a printing press to be used for printing leaflets to distribute in support of the revolution. In February of 1806 he set sail for Venezuela with his expedition. But the Spanish— among them Juan Vicente, Simón Bolívar's brother—were waiting for him as he approached Venezuela. Miranda was able to escape, but two of his ships were captured and ten of his men were hanged. Miranda retreated to the nearby island of Trinidad and then returned to England.

Meanwhile in Europe, Napoleon had his sights set on adding Spain to his territories. He invaded the Iberian Peninsula and, in March 1808, Napoleon forced the Spanish king, Charles IV, to abdicate his crown. Napoleon named his older brother, Joseph Bonaparte, as king of

Spain. But many people in Spanish America rejected Joseph as their ruler. It would be during Joseph's rule of Spain in 1810 that Venezuela would declare independence from the motherland.

Venezuela was the first country in Spanish colonial America to call for independence. In April 1810, the Supreme Junta of Caracas was created. The *junta*, or military group, sent a group to Great Britain to ask for assistance and international recognition as an independent country. Among those in the group was Simón Bolívar. But Great Britain did not offer the support the Venezuelans requested and the trip was cut short. Even still, the trip was a success personally for Bolívar in that he gained experience in diplomacy and negotiations. Before he left England, Bolívar met with Francisco de Miranda, who was in exile, and persuaded him to return to Venezuela. Miranda joined him in their home country one month later.

"God grants victory to perseverance."[3]

After Bolívar returned to Venezuela, the junta gave Bolívar the military rank of lieutenant colonel. He also received the terrible news that his brother, Juan Vicente, had died in a shipwreck returning from buying arms in the United States.

In Caracas, all classes of society had organized for the cause of independence in Venezuela. Bolívar became one of the most vocal members. Those who heard him described him as a passionate speaker with conviction and deeply held beliefs. In one speech he declared: "What we desire is that the union be effective, so that it may give us life in the glorious struggle to achieve our freedom."[4]

The proclamation of independence was signed on July 5, 1811, during Venezuela's First Congress.

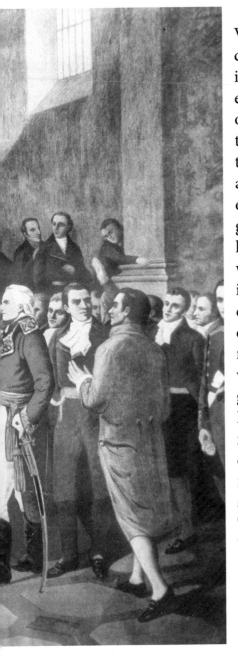

On July 5, 1811, the Venezuelan Congress officially declared the country's independence from Spain and established a republican form of government. In a republic, the people elect representatives to government. Rather than a king or queen, the people elect a president to head the government. Elections were held and a constitution was written and adopted, the first in Spanish America. This constitution ended all legal discrimination based on race; however, full citizenship was only available to a small group of elites in the society. In reality, segregation in the military continued, as did differences in pay based on race. While the slave trade was abolished, slavery continued. The newly formed independent Venezuelan government also agreed to adopt Miranda's tricolor flag as the flag of the republic. The design had three horizontal bands of color: yellow, blue, and red.

THE 1811 VENEZUELAN DECLARATION OF INDEPENDENCE

Written and adopted by the Venezuelan Congress, the Declaration of Independence reads, in part:

[The] United Provinces of Venezuela, calling on the SUPREME BEING to witness the justice of our proceedings and the rectitude of our intentions, do implore his divine and celestial help; and ratifying, at the moment in which we are born to the dignity which his Providence restores to us, the desire we have of living and dying free, and of believing and defending the holy Catholic and Apostolic Religion of Jesus Christ. We, therefore, in the name and by the will and authority which we hold from the virtuous People of Venezuela, DO declare solemnly to the world, that its united Provinces are, and ought to be, from this day, by act and right, Free, Sovereign, and Independent States; and that they are absolved from every submission and dependence on the Throne of Spain, or on those who do, or may call themselves its Agents and Representatives; and that a free and independent State, thus constituted, has full power to take that form of Government which may

be conformable to the general will of the People, to declare war, make peace, form alliances, regulate treaties of commerce, limits, and navigation; and to do and transact every act, in like manner as other free and independent States. And that this, our solemn Declaration, may be held valid, firm, and durable, we hereby mutually bind each Province to the other, and pledge our lives, fortunes, and the sacred tie of our national honor. Done in the Federal Palace of Caracas; signed by our own hands, sealed with the great Provisional Seal of the Confederation, and countersigned by the Secretary of Congress, this 5th day of July, 1811, the first of our Independence." [5]

Since 1811, July 5 is celebrated as Independence Day in Venezuela. Venezuelans typically celebrate this day with military parades, special concerts and festivities, and fireworks.

But the once friendly Bolívar and Miranda soon came to disagreement. Not trusting the Spaniards, Bolívar called for their expulsion from the new republic. Miranda worried that Bolívar's temper was getting the better of him and that widespread expulsion would only make matters worse. When Miranda was asked to take charge of the army by the Executive Council, he agreed to do so only on the condition that Bolívar would not be allowed to serve as an officer in the campaign. The council denied Miranda's request, however.

Francisco de Miranda was imprisoned in Cádiz, Spain, where he died
on July 14, 1816.

Miranda became disillusioned with the state of affairs in his country. Some provinces had remained steadfastly loyal to the Spanish crown. Additionally, when Spain stopped buying Venezuela's main agricultural export, cocoa, it caused financial problems for estate owners and for workers. Many people were not happy with the weakened economy.

Then, in 1812, a powerful earthquake struck northeastern Venezuela resulting in widespread damage and deaths. It is estimated that in Caracas alone, ten thousand people died, with another ten thousand dying in surrounding areas. The earthquake happened during Holy Week, on the Thursday before Easter, called Maundy Thursday in the Catholic religion. Many people were attending services when the earthquake hit and about four thousand died inside churches. Many more died from injuries and wounds days and weeks later. About a week after the initial disaster, another earthquake hit, bringing the number of dead to more than twenty thousand.

Several religious leaders immediately interpreted the catastrophe as a sign from god, as punishment for rebelling against Spain. The archbishop of Caracas, Narciso Coll y Prat, even referred to the event as a "terrifying but well-deserved earthquake".[6] Bolívar rejected the explanation that the earthquake had been the wrath of God as punishment for supporting the revolution. He ran in the streets, sword in hand, trying to rescue as many trapped citizens as he could. When he came upon a monk scolding a crowd for opposing the Spanish crown, Bolívar pulled him down from his platform threatening to kill him if he did not stop his ranting. Bolívar was heard to defiantly say: "If nature oppose us, we will fight against her and force her to obey us."[7]

All of these events led to a weakening of support for the Venezuelan independence movement. Leaders were not in agreement on the best way to proceed. Soldiers of color felt discriminated against. Financial difficulties were felt by all economic classes. And the final blow was the earthquake that devastated Caracas and killed thousands. The First Republic of Venezuela soon collapsed. Miranda observed, "Venezuela is wounded in the heart."[8]

As the Spanish blockaded Venezuela, Miranda disbanded the rebel army. On July 25, 1812, Miranda signed an armistice (a formal agreement to stop fighting) with Domingo Monteverde, the leader of the Spanish military forces. Bolívar and other Venezuelan revolutionary officers thought that it was too soon to give up. They considered Miranda's surrender an act of treason, arrested Miranda, and delivered him to the Spanish Royal Army at the port of La Guaira. Bolívar was granted a passport and he left for Curaçao the next month. Miranda was taken prisoner, sent to Spain, and while awaiting trial, died in a Spanish jail in 1816.

With Miranda no longer heading Venezuela's independence effort, it was at first uncertain who might lead the people. But the answer came soon in the form of Simón Bolívar.

5

The Second Republic

After a brief time on the Caribbean island of Curaçao, Simón Bolívar went to Cartagena, part of a country at the time called New Granada, in December 1812. There he wrote the first of many political texts he would publish in his lifetime. Called the *Cartagena Manifesto*, Bolívar called for the expulsion of all Spanish rulers from Venezuela. He argued that the Venezuelan Constitution was not well-suited to its people, called for a strong stance against enemies, and warned about giving too much authority to dishonest and incompetent leaders. He believed that if these problems could be corrected, Venezuela would be able to achieve independence. He wrote: "Not the Spaniards, but our own disunity has led us back into slavery. A strong government could have changed everything. It would even have been able to master the moral confusion which ensued after the earthquake. With it, Venezuela would today be free."[1] Bolívar also warned New Granada that its own safety was connected to the independence of its nearby neighbor, Venezuela. He called upon New Granada to take up arms in defense of neighboring Venezuela. Following the publication of the *Cartagena Manifesto,* New Granada gave Bolívar two hundred men and permission to enter Venezuela through its border.

This 1812 portrait of Simón Bolívar was painted around the time he wrote the *Cartagena Manifesto*.

Bolívar devised a plan to retake Venezuela. He would start in San José de Cúcuta and end in Caracas, calling it the Campaña Admirable (Admirable Campaign). As Bolívar started off, he knew the next few months would not be easy. The terrain he and his men would have to cross varied from very cold and rainy, to very steep and rugged. In particular, the cordillera (mountain range) of the Andes Mountains was rocky and rough, for both humans and horses. But as Bolívar and his army went from city to city and town to town, more volunteers joined his army, swelling their ranks.

One of the first battles Bolívar's army fought was in Cúcuta, a city located on Venezuela's border with New Granada. There, the Spanish forces totaled one thousand men, many more than in Bolívar's army. But with an aggressive charge, Bolívar's army defeated the Spanish. In their haste to retreat, the Spanish left behind arms and supplies, which Bolívar's army were happy to take for their own use. As they entered the town, local people cheered on Bolívar and his men. For the stunning defeat of the Spanish, the New Granada government promoted Bolívar and rewarded him with the title of brigadier general.

Many people commented on Bolívar's seemingly inexhaustible energy. Daniel O'Leary, an Irish general who served as Bolívar's personal assistant, observed: "After a day's march, enough to exhaust the most robust man, I have seen him work five or six hours, or dance as long."[2] O'Leary kept journals while in the field, most of which survive to the present day. Today, historians agree that Bolívar "slept little and in fact appeared to be in almost perpetual motion. As commander, he became known for

This map depicts South America in 1817.

the custom of dictating orders to two or even more aides simultaneously while he paced the corridor or swung in a hammock. A lover of dancing, he would also attend dances in the towns he passed through on campaign but leave the floor every so often to issue order on some political or military problem, then return to the ball."[3]

As Bolívar's army went through the provinces and cities, they found a mostly supportive people who helped them retake control from the Spanish. In Mucuchíes, in the province of Mérida, Bolívar's men came upon a farm with a large, barking guard dog. Bolívar's men were frightened and wanted to kill the dog, but Bolívar ordered them to put down their swords. The military leader was captivated by the dog's bravery and beauty. The owner of the farm gave the dog as a gift to Bolívar, who named him Nevado (*nieve* means "snow" in Spanish and the name referred to the dog's white fur). For years after, Nevado was inseparable from Bolívar and even fought alongside him during several battles. It was in Mérida that Bolívar was first called "El Libertador" (The Liberator). He declared: "To be the Liberator means more than anything else."[4]

But Bolívar wasn't always so sentimental. When he reached the city of Trujillo in June 1813, Bolívar issued the Decree of War to the Death. In this proclamation, Bolívar declared that Spaniards and criollos would be treated differently. He called for the killing of any Spaniard who did not support the Venezuelan independence cause. Bolívar announced in his decree: "Spaniards and natives of the Canary Islands: Be sure of death even if you are indifferent. Americans: Be sure of life even if you are guilty."[5] He continued to march with his men, triumphantly arriving in Caracas on August 6, 1813, and

PRIMARY SOURCE: CARTAGENA MANIFESTO

The *Cartagena Manifesto* was Bolívar's first public document that he wrote in his quest for Latin American independence. He wrote it after the fall of Venezuela's First Republic, analyzing what went wrong and what he believed should occur in the future. In it, he wrote:

> "[New Granada's] good name depends upon her taking over the task of marching into Venezuela to free that cradle of Colombian independence, its martyrs, and the deserving people of Caracas, whose cries are addressed only to their beloved compatriots, the Granadians, whose arrival, as their redeemers, they await with despairing impatience. Let us hasten to break the chains of those victims who groan in the dungeons, ever hopeful of rescue. Make not a mockery of their trust. Be not insensible to the cries of your brothers. Fly to avenge the dead, to give life to the dying, to bring freedom to the oppressed and liberty to all." [6]

claiming Venezuelan independence. Bolívar's army had marched 800 miles (1,287 kilometers) and groups of girls in white dresses and baskets of flowers greeted them when

DECREE OF WAR TO THE DEATH (PROCLAMATION OF 1813)

Issued in the city of Trujillo, Bolívar's Proclamation of 1813 warned that the murder of Spaniards would be tolerated in the war for independence. By contrast, the lives of South Americans would be spared, even if they had fought on the side of the Spanish crown. He wrote:

"Any Spaniard who does not, by every active and effective means, work against tyranny in behalf of this just cause, will be considered an enemy and punished; as a traitor to the nation, he will inevitably be shot by a firing squad.

On the other hand, a general and absolute amnesty is granted to those who come over to our army ... And you Americans who, by error *or treachery, have been lured from the paths of justice, are informed that your brothers, deeply regretting the error of your ways, have pardoned you as we are profoundly convinced that you cannot be truly to blame, for only the blindness and ignorance in which you have been kept up to now by those responsible for your crimes could have induced you to commit them. Fear not the sword that comes to avenge you and to sever the ignoble ties with which your executioners have bound you to their own fate. You are hereby assured, with absolute impunity, of your honor, lives, and property. The single title, "Americans," shall be your safeguard and guarantee. Our arms have come to protect you, and they shall never be raised against a single one of you, our brothers[...]*

Spaniards and Canary Islanders, you will die, though you be neutral, unless you actively espouse the cause of America's liberation. Americans, you will live, even if you have trespassed." [7]

they arrived. This would be the beginning of Venezuela's Second Republic, but it would not last long.

The following year Bolívar's fortunes would drastically turn for the worse. A financial crisis strained agricultural growers and workers, especially in the important tobacco industry. With disruptions in production and trade, citizens were not able to pay much-needed taxes to the government. Among the people, the pardos still felt

CARABOBO
AYER SE HA
CONFIRMADO
CON UNA
ESPLENDIDA
VICTORIA
EL NACIMIENTO
POLÍTICO DE LA
REPUBLICA
BOLIVAR

A mosaic mural in Caracas, Venezuela, depicts the struggle for Venezuelan independence.

excluded from society, despite being the largest percentage of the Venezuelan population.

In the military realm, Bolívar was challenged by a man named José Tomás Boves. Boves had been born in Spain and was commissioned by the Spanish government to wage war in Venezuela against the independistas (those seeking independence from Spanish rule). He was widely feared for his cruelty and his tendency to execute his enemies without a fair trial. Boves assembled a cavalry of indigenous herders called *llaneros,* so called because they came from the Llanos grasslands east of the Andes Mountains. Boves and his men recaptured Caracas in 1814, which brought the Second Republic of Venezuela to a sudden end.

With the fall of the Second Republic, Bolívar returned to New Granada and eventually made it to the Caribbean island of Jamaica. He lived there from May to December of 1815 with the financial support of an English trader who sympathized with the Spanish American bid for independence. While there, Bolívar petitioned for

British support, trying to convince English officials that South American independence would result in more economic opportunities for Great Britain. The English, while sympathetic, denied his request. In September 1815, Bolívar wrote *La Carta de Jamaica* ("The Jamaica Letter"), explaining why he believed Spanish America should be independent and advocating for a republican form of government fashioned after Great Britain's. He called on Europe to assist in this goal and famously wrote: "More than anyone, I desire to see [South] America fashioned into the greatest nation in the world, greatest not so much by virtue of her area and wealth, as by her freedom and glory."[8]

"It is harder to release a nation from servitude than to enslave a free nation."[9]

While in Jamaica, Bolívar was the target of an assassination attempt. The Spanish had bribed one of Bolívar's former servants, Pío, to kill him. The night of the planned attack, Bolívar was away and one of his officers, José Félix Amestoy, came to receive orders from him. Finding Bolívar gone, the officer fell asleep in Bolívar's hammock, waiting for his return. A case of mistaken identity, Pío attacked and killed Amestoy instead. After escaping this assassination attempt, Bolívar soon left Jamaica for another island nearby.

After the assassination attempt in Jamaica, Bolívar fled to Haiti, where he was given shelter and safety. He arrived in late December 1815, in the seaport town of Aux Cayes, then traveled to Port au Prince, the capital. Haiti had become independent from France in 1803 and was considered a model for the liberation of oppressed people. Alexandre Pétion was elected the first president of Haiti in 1807, and was eventually named president for life. The son of a white French father and a mulatto mother, Pétion became a popular ruler.

Upon arriving in Haiti, Bolívar wrote to Pétion asking to see him. In a letter to his friend Captain Luis Brión, Bolívar expressed that he expected Pétion's "love of liberty and justice" to grant him assistance.[10] Pétion soon took an interest in Bolívar and his plans to liberate Spanish America, and the two became friends. When Bolívar asked the Haitian president for assistance, Pétion obliged, giving him men, armaments, ships, food, and a portable printing press. In exchange for Pétion's military and financial backing, Bolívar vowed to abolish slavery in Spanish America. Although Bolívar was personally against slavery, he knew the Haitian model for independence was a delicate issue in Venezuela and the rest of Latin America. Haiti's liberation had been prompted by a slave revolt that culminated in a revolution. Criollos were worried about the possible violence that a slave rebellion might cause. Bolívar would have to tread carefully on this issue, but he was committed to doing so.

Bolívar also had the assistance of Captain Luis Brión, a native of the Caribbean island of Curaçao. A maritime merchant, Brión had fought in his own country against colonial rule. He was a strong supporter of the Venezuelan independence movement and equipped a ship for battle, giving it to Bolívar for his military campaign. Bolívar was deeply touched by this gift and wrote to him: "I know not what I should most admire in you: your generosity, your patriotism, or your kindness…To you, friend Brión, must be accorded the honor of being the foremost patron of America and the most liberal of men."[11]

With Haiti's backing, Bolívar organized troops to invade Venezuela. Bolívar's flotilla of seven or eight ships carrying soldiers and crew left Aux Cayes, Haiti, in April 1816. Accompanying him was Captain Brión. Their goal was to first reach the island of Margarita off the northeastern coast of Venezuela. Bolívar planned to take advantage of the independence movement that had gained footing there. But before they made it to Margarita Island, Bolívar's ships encountered Spanish warships patrolling the area of the Los Frailes archipelago. In what became known as the naval Battle of Los Frailes, Bolívar's forces soundly defeated the Spanish. For his part in the victory, Brión was named admiral.

Unfortunately, the rest of the campaign would not go as well for the independistas. Bolívar's army was outnumbered by the Spanish Royalists, although a few hundred former slaves joined the independence movement. Remembering Haiti's slave rebellion, criollos were hesitant to support Bolívar, alarmed by his alliance with the ex-slaves. The soldiers, too, were unhappy with their conditions and complained of tainted food rations. Bolívar sent two representatives to Güiria for supplies, but the mission was fruitless.

Bolívar then decided to take matters into his own hands and lead an expedition to Ocumare de la Costa, a small Venezuelan coastal town, where he believed he could round up support, new recruits, and much-needed supplies. But the expedition would prove to be a colossal failure. Bolívar did not find the support he was seeking and morale among officers and soldiers weakened. When they were overtaken by Royalist forces, many of Bolívar's men retreated and abandoned the cause.

With this defeat, Bolívar returned to Haiti to strategize anew. Again, President Pétion lent his assistance and backing. This time Bolívar planned to apply what he had learned from his previous mistakes, making sure his troops were well-outfitted and that he had the support of the people and his officers. He said: "The art of winning is learned in defeat."[12] Bolívar and his expedition, including once again the loyal Brión, left the Haitian port of Jacmel on December 18, 1816. On New Year's Eve, they landed in Barcelona, Venezuela. It was Bolívar's plan to then make their way to the Orinoco River Valley, which he believed was a key and strategic region in the struggle for independence.

Bolívar recruited José Antonio Páez, a caudillo from the Apure Valley, who had experience leading an army of llaneros, the indigenous cowboys from the Llanos grasslands. Páez was so skilled with the llaneros that he earned the nickname "El Centauro de los Llanos" ("The Centaur of the Plains"). In Greek mythology, a centaur is a creature with the head, arms, and torso of a man and the body and legs of a horse. Páez joined forces with Bolívar, contributing one thousand of his men on horseback resulting in an army of four thousand.

In 1817, Bolívar entered Venezuela and set up his military headquarters in the Orinoco River Valley. He captured the city of Angostura (now called Ciudad Bolívar). From there he was able to carry out a number of military campaigns that established his control and power in the region. Two years of fighting followed, with Bolívar's army defeating the Spanish forces at Boyacá, Colombia.

Military scholars hail the Battle at Boyacá as one of the greatest and most surprising victories in history. The

Bolívar was declared president of Gran Colombia when he victoriously returned to Caracas.

llaneros, expert horsemen who were familiar with the rugged terrain of the area, were well prepared for the military campaign that Bolívar had devised. The Spanish could not imagine that rebel forces would be able to cross the inhospitable environment that led to where they were stationed. It was the rainy season and the Apure Valley was flooded, with water sometimes waist-deep as soldiers crossed the plains. The Andean passes were narrow and dangerous, the high altitude made some soldiers sick, and the temperature was bitterly cold. The Spanish forces were not expecting Bolívar's men to make it through the treacherous environment. But the independistas persevered and surprised the Spanish. After only two hours of fighting, the Spanish surrendered. The victory at Boyacá on August 7, 1819, would prove to be an important turning point in the war against the crown.

When Bolívar arrived in Bogotá on August 10, he was cheered and once again called "El Libertador." He called a meeting, the Congress of Angostura, to create a new constitution and government for the Republic of Colombia. Twenty-six delegates gathered at the church in Cúcuta to discuss the new government. Bolívar delivered an impassioned speech in which he described the unique heritage of the criollos: "We are not Europeans; we are not Indians; we are but a mixed species of aborigines and Spaniards. Americans by birth and Europeans by law."[13] He concluded with a forceful call for a strong constitution and a unified society. Bolívar described his vision for the country: "Its principles should be the sovereignty of the people, division of powers, civil liberty, prohibition of slavery, and the abolition of monarchy and privileges."[14]

But it would take another two years for complete independence from Spain to be achieved. Ecuador and Venezuela were still under Spanish rule. During this time, Bolívar joined forces with Francisco de Paula Santander and José Antonio Páez. The Colombian-born Santander had fought in the independence wars of New Granada and was skilled in military maneuvers. The decisive conflict was the 1821 Battle of Carabobo. Bolívar had approached the plains of Carabobo, where the Spanish were camped, from a higher position and was able to look down on them from the top of a hill. From this vantage point, Bolívar was able to see that the army had prepared for an attack from the left and from the center, but not from the right. Taking advantage of this unsecured area, Bolívar ordered an attack on the enemy, taking them by surprise. Sadly, Bolívar's faithful dog, Nevado, died in the battle. Soldiers rushed to Bolívar to give him the news that Nevado was badly injured, but he was not able to arrive until Nevado had already died.

When Bolívar victoriously returned to Caracas, he was declared president of Gran Colombia, an area that included present-day Colombia, Ecuador, Panama, and Venezuela. Francisco de Paula Santander, the military leader who had fought in the independence wars, was named vice president. Bogotá would be the capital of the new republic. But Bolívar was not yet finished; he now set his sights on Ecuador.

Until this point, Spain controlled the Real Audiencia de Quito (the Royal Audience of Quito), an administrative unit of the crown. This area, also called the Presidency of Quito, included modern-day Ecuador and parts of Brazil, Colombia, and Peru. The whole of Ecuador had been staunchly pro-Spanish with one exception: Guayaquil, a thriving port city that had proclaimed its independence from Spain in 1820. The independistas were able to gain support from Gran Colombia and from Argentina. Bolívar took advantage of this support and continued to chip away at Spanish rule.

The following year, a key battle took place on the slopes of the Pichincha volcano on the outskirts of Quito, Ecuador. Bolívar's trusted lieutenant, Antonio José de Sucre, was given command of the campaign. With a force of three thousand recruits and volunteers from several countries, Sucre led his men through difficult terrain. Because of the elevation, many of the soldiers suffered from altitude sickness. The lack of oxygen at high altitude can result in headaches, nausea, and dizziness. Nevertheless, Sucre's army beat the Royalist forces and succeeded in liberating Ecuador in 1822.

By now, only Peru was still controlled by the Spanish. José de San Martín, an Argentinian leader, had been fighting in Peru's liberation movement against the Spanish. Called the "Protector of Peru," San Martín had a long and accomplished military career. Bolívar decided to meet with San Martín at the Conference at Guayaquil. Held in Guayaquil, Ecuador, the two leaders met in private and spoke for many hours about the future of South America. Although the two men had the common goal of independence from colonial rule, they differed greatly on the structure and organization of the government. Bolívar wanted independent nations that would have a republican form of government. San Martín believed that using the European monarchy system made

ANTONIO JOSÉ DE SUCRE

Antonio José de Sucre, Simón Bolívar's trusted military aide, was one of the Libertador's closest friends and most important political advisers. He fought in the independence wars and is considered, along with Bolívar, the liberator of Ecuador and Peru.

Sucre was born to an aristocratic family in Venezuela in 1795. His father was Belgian and had fought for Spain. Sucre's mother was from Spain, the daughter of a Spanish noble. For his military service, Sucre's father was named governor of New Andalucía in Venezuela, arriving in 1779.

Antonio José began his military career at the age of fifteen when he began to fight in the independence wars in Venezuela and Colombia. Sucre's military ability was noted by Bolívar in the 1819 Battle of Boyacá and made him chief of staff in 1820. The two fought alongside each other in the decisive Battle of Carabobo in 1821.

Sucre was known as a skilled military strategist. Despite notoriously difficult terrain and conditions, he led the independistas to victory in the 1822 Battle of Pichincha in Ecuador. Bolívar placed his trust in Sucre in the final campaign for independence, naming Sucre in charge of the battle that took place in the southern city of Ayacucho, Peru. The bloody battle resulted in a sound defeat of the Royalist forces and the creation of the new republic of Peru.

When Bolívar decided to resign as president in January 1830, he was consoled that Sucre was elected president. But that summer, as Bolívar's health was failing, he received the terrible news that Sucre was assassinated returning home to Quito. Sucre died on June 4, 1830. He was thirty-five years old.

Sucre is remembered fondly in the history of Latin America. Bolivia's capital city, Sucre, is named after him. States in Venezuela and in Colombia are named after him as well.

more sense. In the end, the two men were not able to come to an agreement and the conference was deemed a failure. San Martín left for Europe and Bolívar proceeded to his goal of liberating Peru.

In June 1824, Bolívar began moving his army of nine thousand revolutionaries over the Andes Mountains. It was a difficult journey, marching single file up steep mountains with no roads or footpaths, with altitude sickness overcoming many of the soldiers. On August 6, Bolívar and his men reached the hills above the plains of Junín. In a surprise cavalry attack, the independistas struck the Royal Army from the rear. No firearms were used in the ninety-minute battle; the hand-to-hand combat used only lances, spears, sabers, and swords. Bolívar's army handily defeated the Spanish and the Royal Army retreated. Bolívar, proud of the victory, said: "The genius of America led us, and fortune smiled on us. It is not yet a year since I set out from Lima to take fifteen provinces that were in the hands of the renegades...All of this I have achieved without having to fire a single shot."[15]

Bolívar quickly returned to Lima to take control of the government, although the Spanish still had control of southern Peru. Bolívar declared: "I am consumed by the demon of war, determined to finish this struggle."[16] The final battle in the wars for independence would take place in the southern city of Ayacucho, Peru. Once again Bolívar placed his trusted lieutenant, Antonio José de Sucre, in charge of the campaign. It was a bloody battle with many of the Royalist forces killed or taken prisoner. They soon surrendered and Bolívar began the work of establishing the new republic of Peru.

As he had done in other newly liberated countries, Bolívar established several schools, converting convents and monasteries to better serve the youth in the region. In Cuzco, Peru, he ordered the creation of a school for boys by joining two formerly Jesuit schools that had been available only for the elite. A school for girls was also established, unheard of at a time when girls received their education exclusively at home. Before he left Peru, Bolívar arranged for the creation of a hospital for orphans, the elderly, and the disabled.

After the liberation of Peru, the area that was known then as Upper Peru was declared an independent republic. The new republic, Bolivia, was named in honor of "El Libertador." With his strong conviction in the power of education, Bolívar established a new office, the national director of education in the Republic. This position would develop a national curriculum and plan for all public schools. Bolívar believed that the curriculum should focus on the arts and sciences, not on religious instruction as schools had in the past.

"Nations will march towards the apex of their greatness at the same pace as their education. Nations will soar if their education soars; they will regress if it regresses. Nations will fall and sink in darkness if education is corrupted or completely abandoned."[17]

Bolívar's vision was for the independent republics to unite under the broad coalition of Gran Colombia. But he had much work ahead of him to make this dream a reality.

6

Presidente Bolívar

A contemporary of Simón Bolívar described him this way:

"He was not tall...[His] two principal characteristic features...were the excessive mobility of his body and the brilliance of his eyes, which were black, lively, penetrating, and restless, giving him the gaze of an eagle. His hair was black and somewhat curly. His hands and feet were as small as those of a woman, his voice was sharp and penetrating...Those who believe that the man of arms can be recognized by his athletic strength would not have imagined that Bolívar could have achieved what he did."[1]

It was this man who would lead the new country of Gran Colombia in independence.

Bolívar had strong beliefs about Gran Colombia and the way it should be governed. He used ideas from the American Revolution, admiring the democratic values the founders built into the US Constitution. He was especially impressed by the way Thomas Jefferson and others advocated for the education of the common man. Bolívar believed that his own country's "principles should be the sovereignty of the people, division of powers,

Bolívar wanted a unified Latin America.

civil liberty, prohibition of slavery, and the abolition of monarchy and privileges. We need equality…a unified nation, all classes of men, political opinions, and public customs."[2]

"During my brief visit to the United States I saw rational liberty for the first time in my life."[3]

But Bolívar was unsure if the American model could be fully applied in Latin America. Bolívar believed that Latin American independence would require a stronger government than that instituted in the United States. The North and South American continents had different histories, cultures, and peoples. Bolívar said that Spanish America had been "enslaved by the triple yoke of ignorance, tyranny, and vice" and that "an ignorant people is the blind instrument of its own destruction."[4] In the speech he had given at the Angostura Congress in 1819, he questioned the people's ability to govern themselves under the current conditions. He quoted Jean-Jacques Rousseau, the Enlightenment thinker he had studied while in Europe: "Liberty, says Rousseau, is a succulent morsel, but one difficult to digest. Our weak fellow-citizens will have to strengthen their spirit greatly before they can digest the wholesome nutriment of freedom."[5]

Bolívar also did not agree with the system of slavery in the United States, saying that "slavery is the daughter of darkness."[6] Although Bolívar and his family owned slaves, he was fervently antislavery and worked hard to eliminate the system in Spanish America. He believed that children born to slaves "should be free, for these creatures belong only to God and to their parents, and neither God nor their parents wish them to be unhappy."[7] Bolívar believed he was free of racial prejudice and advocated equality for all people. At a time when whites and blacks were kept strictly apart, he even dared to make the declaration that a more equal and just society could be achieved with race mixing. He said: "The blood of our citizens is diverse; let us mix it to make it one."[8] Among the immediate actions Bolívar took as president, he outlawed slavery. It gave him great satisfaction that among the freed slaves was his childhood nurse, Hipólita. In 1824 he struck down all remaining slavery laws, granting blacks "all possible protection of the government."[9]

Bolívar took all of his ideas of what would make a successful government and proposed a division of powers. People would have the right to elect representatives, but the president would be appointed for life by the legislature. He argued that until the new republic was well established, having a permanent presidency would provide stability. Bolívar said, "elections would be avoided, which are the greatest scourge of republics and produce only anarchy."[10] The president would also have the right to appoint his successor when he died or had to leave office. Bolívar insisted that these measures were necessary to ensure liberty for all. But others criticized the strong role the central government would play. They challenged Bolívar's contention that the president would be "the sun which, fixed in its orbit, imparts life to the universe."[11]

During this time Bolívar also met a woman who would become a very important figure in his life. Bolívar had been devastated when his young bride died in 1803 after arriving in Venezuela and vowed to never remarry.

Manuela Sáenz was Bolívar's confidante and the final great love of his life.

He kept this vow, but had female companions over the years. Historians believe that during his time in Quito, after consolidating Peru's independence, he met the final great love of his life, Manuela Sáenz.

When Bolívar had marched triumphantly into Quito he was enthusiastically greeted by the people, who had decorated their homes in the red, blue, and gold colors of the Gran Colombia flag. They flooded the streets and watched from their balconies as Bolívar's procession went by, hailing the Liberator. The festivities continued that evening with a ball at the home of a well-to-do family. It was at this event that Bolívar and Sáenz would meet.

Sáenz was a devoted revolutionary dedicated to the independence cause. Outspoken and strong-willed, she championed women's rights in a time and place where women stayed home. Sáenz was considered a great beauty, described as "attractive and shapely, her oval face, pearl complexion, dark eyes and flowing hair the epitome of South American beauty."[12] She was also a skilled fighter, handling both sword and pistol with self-confidence.

After they met in 1822, Sáenz and Bolívar were inseparable. In a letter to her, Bolívar wrote: "Everything in you is love. I too am suffering from this searing fever which consumes us as though we were two children."[13] One of Bolívar's biographers wrote of their close relationship: "If he was angry, she calmed him. If he was sad, she enlivened him. She could share with him the coarseness of camp life or move in society like a great lady. She used to read to him, particularly at night, and she cared for him when he was ill."[14] Later, Sáenz accompanied Bolívar to Bogotá, the capital of Gran Colombia where the presidential palace was established.

MANUELA SÁENZ

Manuela Sáenz was a precocious child and her strong personality was evident early on. When her mother died at a young age, she was sent to the Convent of Santa Catalina. Instead of praying and minding her church lessons, Sáenz smoked cigars, danced, and secretly dated a Spanish officer. For this behavior, she was expelled from the convent and was moved to Panama by her father. In Panama she met a wealthy British merchant twenty years older than her. The two married in 1817, but it was a marriage of convenience. When Sáenz and Bolívar met, even though Sáenz was a married woman, the two fell in love.

Just like when she was a child, Manuela's sharp sense of humor sometimes got her into trouble as an adult. She sometimes dressed in men's clothing so she could move about society more freely. When Bolívar was president, Sáenz was blamed for organizing a mock execution of one of Bolívar's enemies, Francisco de Paula Santander. Making a life-size doll representing Santander, partygoers put him to death with a simulated firing squad. When the incident was brought to Bolívar's attention, he confronted Sáenz, but she denied knowledge of having orchestrated the event. Bolívar tolerated her antics, affectionately calling her *mi amable loca* (my sweet crazy woman).

Sáenz lived for twenty-six years after Bolívar's death. She died of diphtheria in 1856. In an effort to contain the spread of the disease at the time, Sáenz was buried in a mass grave alongside other victims of the epidemic. But, in 2010, she was given an official state burial in Venezuela. Although none of her remains were recoverable, a symbolic reburial, made up of soil taken from the mass grave took place in the National Pantheon in Venezuela, near Bolívar's remains.

Bolívar still had hopes that he would be able to join the countries of the Americas into a cohesive whole. He declared: "The great day of America has not yet dawned. We have expelled our oppressors, broken the tables of their tyrannical laws and founded legitimate institutions. But we still need to establish the basis of the social compact, which ought to form of this world a nation of republics."[15] In December 1824, Bolívar invited governments throughout Latin America to send representatives to a meeting that would be held in Panama. Bolívar explained his choice of location: "It seems that if the world had to choose its capital, the Isthmus of Panama would be chosen for that privileged purpose, positioned as it is in the center of the globe, looking at Asia on one side and at Africa and Europe on the other."[16] The United States and key European nations were also invited. The purpose of the Congress of Panama was to establish an alliance of South American republics that would trade, work together, and defend each other militarily. But representatives from only four countries made it to the meeting. The gathering was not successful and the countries were not able to come to the agreements Bolívar had envisioned.

Discontent in the republics increased and the local governments became unstable. Nowhere was this truer than in Bolívar's native Venezuela. As local officials argued about how best to lead the country to recovery, many people thought that the central government had too much power. But Bolívar believed that the opposite was true. He argued that the central government had to take a more active role in governing the people and bringing stability to the republics. On August 27, 1828, Bolívar issued the Organic Decree of Dictatorship. Through this measure, he proclaimed himself dictator, a ruler who has total power over a country, and eliminated the country's vice president. He said this would only be temporary—until a congress was convened in January 1830—but that it was needed to save the republic. Bolívar declared: "I earnestly desire to improve the fate of the people of Venezuela...they are so miserable that it is essential to relieve their suffering at any price."[17] Some historians agree, pointing out that Bolívar's new position was not a traditional dictatorship. One scholar believes that Bolívar "did not destroy the permanence of institutions nor did he flaunt the law or refuse to listen to popular will".[18]

But the Organic Decree was seen as heavy-handed and angered his enemies. Many years later, a Venezuelan historian concluded that Bolívar made a mistake in issuing the decree, stating that it "was something he [Bolívar] paid for deliberately with unpopularity, with his dying, and with his death."[19] Because his unpopular decree generated such discontent and opposition, it affected Bolívar greatly, impacting both his physical health and his emotional state. Bolívar lamented in 1828: "All America resounds with complaints about me."[20]

Arquitectura colonial _ Plazuela Rufino Cuervo _ Al fondo destácanse las cúpulas de la Capilla del Sagrario y de la Catedral Primada _ Bogotá _ Colombia _

San Carlos Plaza is near the palace where an attempt was made on Bolívar's life in 1828.

The following month there was an attempt on Bolívar's life while he was at the Palacio de San Carlos in Bogotá. A group made up of military officers, law school students, and local merchants, angry at some of Bolívar's measures, plotted to kill him as he slept. Although Bolívar had heard rumblings of assassination plots, he did not take them seriously and did not believe he was in immediate danger.

On the evening of September 25, 1828, Bolívar felt ill and called Manuela Sáenz to his side. She took care of him, including reading to him, until he fell asleep. But shortly after midnight, she heard some strange noises and dogs barking in the presidential palace. She woke up Bolívar, got him dressed, and persuaded him to escape through a window. As the assassins entered Bolívar's bedroom, they found Sáenz with a sword in her hand. The men demanded that she tell them where Bolívar was. Sáenz told them he was in a meeting in another room in the palace. Then some of them noticed that Bolívar's bed was still warm and that there was an open window. Sáenz lied, saying that the warm bed was because she had been lying on it while waiting for Bolívar to return from his meeting. She said she had opened the window because of the dogs' barking.

The assassins spared Sáenz's life, but she sustained wounds that took weeks to heal. When the assassins realized that Bolívar had escaped through the open window, they went outside to try to find him. Bolívar met up with one of his loyal servants, José Palacios, and together they hid under a bridge that spanned the San Agustín River, which served as one of Bogotá's sewers. After many cold and wet hours in hiding, Bolívar and Palacios were finally able to come out of hiding and into safety. After the thwarted assassination attempt, Bolívar began calling Sáenz the "liberator of the liberator."

Following the attack, sixty people were rounded up for questioning, including Vice President Francisco de Paula Santander. Fourteen men were ultimately arrested and found guilty of conspiring against the president. For their actions, they were sentenced to death by firing squad. Bolívar pardoned Santander and sent him into exile. But some people criticized the way the government investigated the attack and charged that the sentences were unfairly applied to some citizens and not others.

"Those who serve a revolution plow the sea."[21]

Dissatisfaction with Bolívar's Gran Colombia government grew and uprisings continued in New Granada, Ecuador, and Venezuela over the next two years. Some slave owners were dissatisfied with the law of emancipation set by the new congress. Citizens in New Granada complained they were not represented fairly in the central government. Venezuelans pointed out that there were few of them who held office in key government positions. Others charged that the new government was as corrupt as the one before. This widespread discontent resulted in Venezuela seceding (withdrawing formally) from Gran Colombia in late 1829. Soon after, Ecuador seceded, too. Bolívar realized that opposition to his vision of government prevented him from effectively leading the people. On January 20, 1830, Bolívar convened a congress and submitted his resignation as president. In a proclamation, he sadly declared: "Today I have ceased to lead you."[22] He took some comfort that military leader Antonio José de Sucre, who had fought alongside Bolívar in the wars for independence, was elected president.

7

The Passing of El Libertador

After resigning from the presidency, Simón Bolívar intended to go to Europe. However, his health was failing and it was clear he could not endure a long ocean voyage. He was very tired, had lost a large amount of weight, and had a persistent cough. Bolívar decided to move instead to a more temperate climate, hoping it would improve his health. He settled on Santa Marta in northern Colombia near the Caribbean Sea. Instead of sailing to Europe, he would take an unhurried journey on the Magdalena River to arrive at his destination.

Historians are unsure why Manuela Sáenz was not able to accompany Bolívar on this final trip. As he left Bogotá, Bolívar wrote a farewell letter to her, advising her to be careful. He wrote: "I love you, my love, but I will love you even more if you show great prudence, now more than ever."[1] The two lovers would never see each other again.

As Bolívar's boat made its way on the Magdalena River, they would stop at towns and cities along the way. When he arrived in Cartagena in the summer of 1830, he was received with a hero's welcome, which lifted his spirits. But in Cartagena he received the devastating news that his friend and political successor, Antonio José Sucre, had been assassinated. Sucre had been attending a convention

...CUERDA LOS HECHOS HEROICOS VENERANDO A SU LIBERTAD

This 1830 portrait of Bolívar in Bogotá was painted by artist José Gil de Castro.

on the future of Colombia. As he was returning home to Quito, unescorted in a mountainous region, he was ambushed and killed. Bolívar became depressed and sunk further into despair as his health worsened. He reported on his weakened state: "My illness is getting worse, and I am so weak that this very day I suffered a dreadful fall; I fell down without knowing how, and I was half-dead."[2]

As his health failed, so did Bolívar's faith in the future of Latin America. In a letter he wrote to Venezuelan General Juan José Flores, who had become the first president of Ecuador, Bolívar expressed his frustration and hopelessness:

> *You know that I have ruled for twenty years, and from these I have derived only a few certainties: (1) America is ungovernable, for us; (2) Those who serve a revolution plough [plow] the sea; (3) The only thing one can do in America is emigrate.*[3]

As his boat continued on the Magdalena, his anguish only increased.

Bolívar finally arrived in Santa Marta on December 1, 1830. He retained Dr. Alejandro Próspero Révérend to care for him. On December 6, Bolívar was moved to a country house, called the Quinta of Saint Peter of Alexandria, in order to rest. At first, the Liberator's condition seemed to improve in his new environment, but the improvement was short lived. A Colombian general who saw Bolívar toward the end of his life described his failing health: "He was pale, drawn, and his eyes, so brilliant and expressive in his good days, were already dull; his deep voice was hardly audible."[4]

As his health failed, Bolívar became more despondent over the future of Latin America.

As his condition worsened, a priest was called to perform the last rites of the Catholic religion. These sacraments were given on December 10—the same day the Liberator signed his last will and testament. Bolívar also wrote a letter in which he said: "My last wishes are for the happiness of our native land. If my death will help to end party strife and to consolidate the Union, I shall go to my grave in peace."[5] He was despondent over the status of Latin America. Shortly before his death, Bolívar exclaimed, "Jesus Christ, Don Quixote de la Mancha, and I have been the world's three greatest fools."[6]

On December 17, 1830, with his doctor and trusted assistants by his side, the Liberator took his last breath. Dr. Révérend reported that his death was peaceful. The cause of death recorded was tuberculosis. Bolívar was forty-seven.

Bolívar was originally buried in the nearby Cathedral of Santa Marta, after a formal funeral and procession. But a few years later, the Venezuelan government petitioned to bury Bolívar in his home country. In 1842, Bolívar's remains were moved to Caracas. According to legend, Bolívar's heart and other vital organs were placed in an urn and left in the Santa Marta Cathedral by the Venezuelan officials who had come to claim the remains. The officials explained that the Venezuelan people were grateful for the home and support Colombia had offered Bolívar in his dying days and left the Liberator's organs as a testament of this gratitude.

In 1875, the National Pantheon was established in Caracas in a former church. The National Pantheon is the final resting place of Venezuelan heroes. Famous writers, politicians, and military leaders are buried there. The Venezuelan president Antonio Guzmán Blanco declared,

A DEADLY DISEASE

In the nineteenth century, tuberculosis was a common illness but little was known about its causes. It was a leading cause of death, especially among city dwellers. In English-speaking countries it was also called "consumption," reflecting the gradual wasting away of its victims. By the end of the century, medical researchers had identified the bacterial origin of the disease, but an effective cure had still not been found.

The tuberculosis bacterium, *Mycobacterium tuberculosis*, usually attacks the lungs but it can affect other body organs, too. When an infected person talks, coughs, or sneezes, the disease spreads to others through the air. Tuberculosis symptoms include a recurring cough with blood or mucus, extreme fatigue, loss of appetite, weight loss, and high fever. Simón Bolívar experienced all of these symptoms.

Today, doctors can determine if a patient has tuberculosis by performing blood and skin tests and taking X-rays of the lungs. Effective medicines have been discovered and developed that can usually cure the disease. During Bolívar's lifetime, neither the tests nor the medicines existed.

POISONED?

In 2010, the cause of Bolívar's death was revisited when Dr. Paul Auwaerter, an infectious diseases expert at the Johns Hopkins School of Medicine in Baltimore, Maryland, proposed an alternate theory about how the Liberator died. Dr. Auwaerter suggested that Bolívar's symptoms when he died were more consistent with arsenic poisoning than with tuberculosis. He noted that at the time, arsenic was used as a medicine for many ailments and that many of the Andean rivers also had unusually high arsenic levels.

Venezuela's president Hugo Chávez had been convinced for many years that the Liberator had been murdered. The arsenic theory seemed to prove his point. So, in July 2010, under Chávez's orders, Bolívar's coffin was opened and his skeleton was removed. Chávez was present at the exhumation, overcome with emotion. He tweeted: "My God. Bolívar lives. It's not a skeleton. It's the Great Bolívar, who has returned."[8]

Many tests were conducted on Bolívar's remains by forensic scientists. After a year of study, all that the scientists could find were small traces of toxins in the skeletal remains. Although arsenic was found, scientists concluded that there was no evidence of intentional poisoning.

"It is not enough that Venezuela's heroes be preserved for posterity on the pages of history. Their ashes should be guarded with religious respect, in this manner insuring an everlasting monument of national gratitude."[7] In 1876, Bolívar's remains were transferred to the National Pantheon, where they remain to this day. In the center of the building is a special area dedicated entirely to Bolívar. With soldiers standing guard, the Liberator's bronze casket is accented with a beautiful crystal chandelier hanging above that was mounted in 1883, on the one hundredth anniversary of Bolívar's birth.

8

Bolívar's Legacy

S imón Bolívar famously said, "God grants victory to perseverance."[1] It was perseverance—persistently working at something with determination—that perhaps best marks the Liberator's military and political career. Despite personal tragedies, military setbacks,

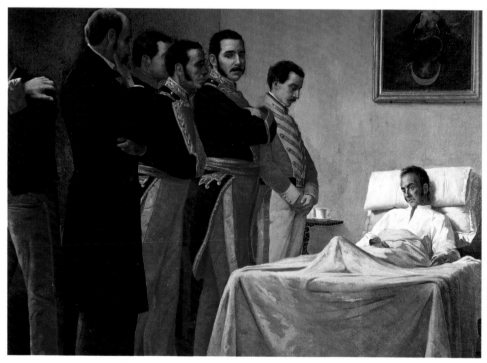

This painting by Venezuelan artist Antonio Herrera Toro depicts Bolívar's death.

and political opposition, Bolívar held on to his dream of a free and united South America. All in all, Bolívar participated in nearly one hundred battles and 80,000 miles (128,748 km) of military marches, an astounding feat.[2] Although his vision of a united South America would not become a reality, he was nonetheless able to realize the liberation of six countries from colonial rule. He is credited with being the liberator of New Granada (Colombia, 1819), Panama and Venezuela (1821); Ecuador (1822); Peru (1824); and Bolivia (1825).

BOLÍVAR AND THE PANTHEON OF HEROES

For his military and political achievements, many people consider Bolívar a hero. Venezuelan artist Arturo Michelena immortalized Bolívar in his oil painting *The Pantheon of Heroes* in 1898. In it, Venezuelan heroes are assembled at a Greek temple with Bolívar occupying the honored seat directly below a statue of the goddess Nike. On the right of the painting, Liberty is on horseback slaying a lion, a symbol of bloodthirsty domination over the innocent.

Michelena completed *The Pantheon of Heroes* just a few months before he died of tuberculosis at the young age of thirty-five in 1898. For his contribution to Venezuelan culture, Arturo Michelena's remains were buried in the National Pantheon in 1948.

Although it will soon be two hundred years since Simón Bolívar died, the impact of his vision and legacy is still evident throughout Latin America and around the world. Throughout the Americas, many places bear his name. There is the country of Bolivia, as well as many towns, cities, and provinces throughout the continent. The currency in Venezuela, Bolívar's birth country, is the Venezuelan bolívar. The international airport is also named after him, as are many plazas, parks, and streets.

Bolívar is so highly regarded that there are a number of statues of him throughout the world. In Europe, there are parks, plazas, and streets named after the Liberator. Canada has statues of Bolívar in Toronto and Ottawa. Europe boasts several monuments in Austria, England, France, Germany, and Spain. Statues of Bolívar can also be found

This monument to Simón Bolívar stands in New York City's
Central Park.

in Egypt and Iran. In the United States, cities such as New York; Washington, DC; New Orleans; San Francisco; and Miami, Florida; all have monuments in honor of the Liberator.

The United States also has cities and counties named after him. A high school in Bolívar, Missouri, calls itself "The Home of the Liberators."[3] There was even a US general, Simon Bolívar Buckner, who fought in the Mexican-American War and the US Civil War. His parents named him after the South American Liberator who was popular and well known throughout the Americas when Buckner was born in 1823. Simon Bolívar Buckner was later elected governor of Kentucky. He named his son Simon Bolívar Buckner Jr., who went on to serve in the US Army during World War II.

There are other connections between Bolívar and the United States. Historians have made comparisons between Bolívar and George Washington. The two leaders had many things in common, including losing their parents at a young age. Neither had extensive military training yet went on to victoriously lead their armies against colonial rule. Since both military leaders are credited with leading their countries to independence, Bolívar is sometimes referred to as the "George Washington of South America." While Bolívar was alive, he was presented with a miniature portrait of Washington, along with a lock of his hair, by the North American leader's family who called Bolívar "the second Washington of the New World."[4] The memento was brought to Bolívar by the Marquis de Lafayette, a French military officer who had fought in the American Revolution. Lafayette said that "of all men living, and even of all men in history, Bolívar is the very one to whom my paternal friend would have preferred to send this present."[4] It is said that Bolívar wore the miniature "constantly, in admiration of Washington."[5] The Liberator believed that "Washington, hand in hand with Lafayette, is the crown of all human rewards."

More recently, the Liberator inspired the Twenty-First Century Bolívarian Revolution, a political movement created by Hugo Chávez. Chávez was a Venezuelan military officer and politician who was elected president of the country in 1998, promising social reforms and a more participatory democratic system. Chávez was an admirer of Bolívar, having studied his life, military career, and political writings. He even renamed the country the Bolívarian Republic of Venezuela. Borrowing language from the Monte Sacro oath Bolívar made in Italy in 1805, Chávez declared: "I swear by the God of my fathers, I swear by my honor, and I swear by my homeland that I shall give no respite to my arm nor rest to my soul until we have broken the chains that the powerful have placed upon us."[6] As president, when he appeared on television Chávez often spoke in front of a portrait of Bolívar. The country's constitution approved in 1999 included this statement: "The Bolivian Republic of Venezuela…bases its moral authority and its values of freedom, equality, justice, and international peace on the doctrine of Simón Bolívar, the Liberator."[7] Although Chávez's presidency was popular at the beginning of his term, by 2010 he faced significant opposition as the economy weakened and government corruption grew.

"I swear before you; I swear by the God of my fathers; I swear by my fathers; I swear

on my honor; and I swear by my country
that I will not rest body or soul until I have
broken the chains with which Spanish
power oppresses us."[8]

Bolívar's life has also inspired works of art. In 1989, Nobel Prize–winning author Gabriel García Márquez published *The General in His Labyrinth*. The novel is a fictionalized retelling of Bolívar's last days as he traveled to Santa Marta, reflecting on his successes and failures. It is an unsentimental look at the last seven months of Bolívar's life, recounting both his physical deterioration as well as imagining his thoughts about his inability to unite the continent.

Bolívar's life has also made it to the silver screen. A Spanish-Venezuelan film on Bolívar's life was released in 2013. Starring Venezuelan actor Edgar Ramírez in the title role, the historical drama was shown at the 2013 Toronto International Film Festival to great acclaim. Venezuela selected the film as its entry in the Best Foreign Language Film at the 2015 Academy Awards. Although the film did not win, it introduced new audiences to the life of Bolívar.

Every two years the United Nations Educational, Scientific, and Cultural Organization (UNESCO) awards the International Simón Bolívar Prize. Created in 1945 on the heels of two world wars, UNESCO promotes peace and understanding among the world's people through education and scientific cooperation. The International Simón Bolívar Prize recognizes activities that are in keeping with Bolívar's ideals, namely, "freedom, independence and dignity of peoples and to the strengthening of a new international economic, social

SIMÓN BOLÍVAR: THE OPERA

In 1995, an opera based on Bolívar's life was performed across the United States and Europe. Simply titled *Simón Bolívar*, it was commissioned by the Los Angeles Music Center Opera and the Scottish Opera. It premiered at the Virginia Opera in Norfolk. Written by Scottish composer Thea Musgrave, the work incorporated actual gunfire and used powerful, driving music to capture a sense of the real-life drama at the time. The lyrics were originally composed in English but translated and sung in Spanish. Theatergoers were given translations so they could understand the storyline.

The opera ends with Bolívar singing these words:

Freedom: the fierce, unending battle
against tyranny, against anarchy.
Freedom demands your heart,
your mind, your imagination,
and even your very life.
That is the heavy price for
one brief moment of glory.[9]

and cultural order."[10] An international jury of seven must unanimously agree on the winner. Nelson Mandela, the South African anti-apartheid leader, received the award in 1983. Bangladeshi Muhammad Yunus won the award in 1996 for his pioneering work in microcredit, loans given to businesspeople too poor to qualify for traditional bank loans. The prize is always awarded on July 24, Bolívar's birthday.

Today we know a lot about Bolívar's life and his beliefs because he left a rich store of writings. He was a prolific writer according to one historian: "He wrote everyone, all the time, about everything. Dictating to three scribes at the same time, three different letters on three different subjects, Bolívar's verbal creativity produced a torrent of documents in a short time that even today...amazes us with its volume and variety."[11] Bolívar had asked his personal assistant, General Daniel O'Leary, to burn all of his personal documents upon his death, but O'Leary disobeyed those orders. O'Leary himself also kept detailed journals and these too have helped historians piece together Bolívar's life

Bolívar died penniless, with most of his properties having been sold years before. He is remembered as unfailingly generous, helping those in need and even going into debt as he helped others. He was particularly concerned with single mothers who lost their husbands in combat and orphans who lost their parents to wars and illness. During his lifetime, he established several schools for poor children, often converting former monasteries and convents. Bolívar was also concerned about the elderly and disabled and created hospitals for their care.

One of Bolívar's biographers, Marie Arana, was asked what made him such a gifted leader. Arana responded: "He had a tremendous talent for bringing people together and making warring generals cooperate. He would co-opt them personally, he would charm them, he would engage them. He was very bright. He was tremendously impressive both intellectually and physically."[12] Many years after the Liberator's death, he is remembered as someone with the vision to liberate the people of Latin America from colonial rule.

CONCLUSION

Although Bolívar's dream of a unified coalition of Latin American countries did not materialize, his vision and efforts resulted in several independent nations and paved the way for a more democratic region.

After three hundred years of colonial rule, most of Latin America had declared its independence from Spain and Portugal by 1830. The first uprising against the Spanish crown is credited to Ecuador, in 1809. Over the next two decades, more countries declared their independence and went to war against their colonial rulers. With the lone exceptions of Cuba and Puerto Rico, Latin America and the Caribbean emerged as a region of independent nations by 1830. The ideas of the Enlightenment were evident in many of the constitutions being drafted in these new countries. "Natural rights" such as liberty, equality, and personal property were guaranteed in writing, although not all citizens enjoyed full social and economic equality until the following century. The last two countries to finally abolish slavery were Cuba (1886) and Brazil (1888).

During the late 1800s these new Latin American governments struggled to meet the needs of their growing populations. As the Industrial Revolution introduced railroads, steam engines, machines that ran on natural gas, and electrical systems, the young countries borrowed large sums of money from foreign governments incurring hefty debts. In turn, exportation of natural resources such as wood, rubber, and minerals was increased. While these exports brought in much-needed capital, the massive amount of exports also resulted in the devastation of many natural environments in the region.

With industrialization came urbanization, especially in the early part of the 1900s. Like in other parts of the world, huge numbers of people moved from rural areas into cities. Urban population growth was also impacted by immigration from other countries. Political and social upheaval as a result of World War I (1914-1918) and World War II (1939-1945) resulted in the region experiencing immigration from other countries. Countries such as Argentina, Brazil, and Cuba received millions of new citizens during this time.

The twentieth century saw the rise of dictatorships in several Latin American countries and, increasingly, challenges to those dictatorships. The revolution in Russia in the first half of the century had an impact in Latin America as socialist parties sprung up and demanded political, social, and economic reforms. In some countries, such as Bolivia and Cuba, these reform efforts had an impact in the redistribution of land and businesses. Other countries' socialist-leaning governments, like those in Chile and Nicaragua, were overthrown after internal and external challenges.

Today, Latin America is considered to be a largely democratic region, with Cuba being the only remaining dictatorship. Far from being "ungovernable" as Bolívar once feared, the region is home to many democratically elected governments. Although Latin America as a whole does not enjoy the economic prosperity of the Northern Hemisphere, there are reasons to be hopeful for the region. It has a young population, better educated and informed than in generations past. This new citizenry will demand a voice in government and strive to improve their societies. Bolívar's vision might come to fruition after all.

CHRONOLOGY

3   Simón Bolívar is born on July 24 in Caracas, Venezuela.

6   Simón's father, Juan Vicente, dies.

2   Simón's mother, María de la Concepción, dies.

7   Bolívar enrolls in the military academy Milicias de Aragua.

9   He travels to Europe to continue his studies; lives there for three years.

2   Bolívar marries María Teresa Rodríguez del Toro y Alaiza; the couple moves to Venezuela.

3   María Teresa dies.

3   Bolívar travels to Europe and spends nearly four years there.

5   He takes a vow to liberate Latin America on Monte Sacro in Rome, Italy.

6   Francisco de Miranda fails in his attempt to liberate Venezuela.

7   Bolívar returns to Venezuela.

8   Napoleon Bonaparte forces the Spanish king, Charles IV, to abdicate and names his brother, Joseph Bonaparte, as king of Spain.

1   The Venezuelan Congress officially declares the country's independence from Spain.

2   A powerful earthquake strikes Venezuela, killing thousands and causing widespread damage; Bolívar writes the *Cartagena Manifesto*.

3   Bolívar begins the Campaña Admirable culminating in the Second Republic of Venezuela; issues the Decree of War to the Death.

1814 The Second Republic of Venezuela comes to an end; Bolívar flees to New Granada.

1815 Bolívar writes the *Carta de Jamaica* and becomes the target of an assassination attempt.

1816 He secures the support of Haitian president Alexandre Petión.

1817 Bolívar enters Venezuela and sets up his military headquarters in the Orinoco River Valley.

1819 He defeats Spanish forces at Boyacá; calls the Congress of Angostura to create a new constitution; and is elected president of the Third Republic of Venezuela.

1821 Bolívar defeats the Spanish in the Battle of Carabobo and is named president of a new republic, Gran Colombia.

1822 Bolívar meets Manuela Sáenz; Ecuador is liberated from Spanish rule.

1824 Bolívar calls the Congress of Panamá with the purpose of establishing an alliance of South American republics; Peru is liberated from Spanish rule.

1825 A new republic, Bolivia, is established and named in honor of Bolívar.

1828 Bolívar issues the Organic Decree of Dictatorship; a second assassination attempt is thwarted.

1830 As dissatisfaction with Bolívar grows, he submits his resignation as president; he dies and is buried in Santa Marta, Colombia, on December 17.

1842 Bolívar's remains are moved to
      Caracas, Venezuela.

1875 The National Pantheon is established in
      Caracas, Venezuela.

1876 Bolívar's remains are transferred to the
      National Pantheon.

2010 Bolívar's remains are exhumed under the
      order of Venezuelan president Hugo Chávez,
      in order to determine if Bolívar was poisoned;
      there is no evidence found to suggest this.

Chapter Notes

Chapter 1: Love and Loss

1. John Lynch, *Simón Bolívar: A Life* (New Haven, CT: Yale University Press, 2006), p. 19.

2. Lynch, p. 21.

Chapter 2: A Venezuelan Childhood

1. Gerhard Masur, *Simón Bolívar* (Albuquerque, NM: University of New Mexico Press, 1969), p. 21.

2. Augusto Mijares, *The Liberator* (Caracas, Venezuela: North American Association of Venezuela, 1991), p.2.

3. Richard W. Slatta and Jane Lucas De Grummond, *Simón Bolívar's Quest for Glory* (College Station, TX: Texas A&M University Press, 2003), p. 12.

4. Mijares, p.4.

5. Simón Bolívar, "Message to the Congress of Angostura, 1819," Fordham University. Retrieved December 22, 2016. http://sourcebooks.fordham.edu/mod/1819bolivar.asp.

6. Masur, pp. 25-26.

7. Mijares, p.37.

Chapter 3: Travels in Europe

1. John Lynch, *Simón Bolívar: A Life* (New Haven, CT: Yale University Press, 2006), p. 21.

2. Gerhard Masur, *Simón Bolívar* (Albuquerque, NM: University of New Mexico Press, 1969), p. 34.

3. Augusto Mijares, *The Liberator* (Caracas, Venezuela: North American Association of Venezuela, 1991), p. 4.

4. Lynch, p. 93.

6. Lynch, p. 25.

7. Bolívar as quoted in Lester D. Langley, *Simón Bolívar: Venezuelan Rebel, American Revolutionary* (New York, NY: Rowman & Littlefield Publishers, 2009), p. 15.

8. Ian A. Freeman, *Seeds of Revolution: A Collection of Axioms, Passages and Proverbs, Volume 1* (Bloomington, IN: iUniverse, 2014).

9. Lynch, p. 25.

10. Mark A. Burkholder and D.S. Chandler, *From Impotence to Authority* (Columbia, MO: University of Missouri Press, 1977), pp. 191-192.

11. Lynch, p. 27.

12. William R. Manning, *The Independence of the Latin American Nations (1923)*, p. 1322, as quoted in Augusto Mijares, p. 115.

Chapter 4: Independence for Venezuela

1. Karen Stolley, "Writing Back to Empire: Juan Pablo Viscardo y Guzmán's 'Letter to the Spanish Americans,'" *American Antiquarian Society*, 2007, p. 1.

2. Gerhard Masur, *Simón Bolívar* (Albuquerque, NM: University of New Mexico Press, 1969), pp. 21-22.

3. Lester D. Langley, *Simón Bolívar: Venezuelan Rebel, American Revolutionary* (New York, NY: Rowman & Littlefield Publishers, 2009), p. 51.

4. Langley, p. 33.

5. "Declaration of Independence of Venezuela—July 5, 1811," Declaration Project. Retrieved December 22, 2016. http://www.eclarationproject.org/?p=370.

6. "Nacimiento de una nación: Terremoto de 1812," Revolvy, 2006. https://www.revolvy.com/main/index.php?s=1812%20Caracas%20earthquake.

7. Richard W. Slatta and Jane Lucas De Grummond, *Simón Bolívar's Quest for Glory* (College Station, TX: Texas A&M University Press, 2003), p. 56.

8. John Lynch, *Simón Bolívar: A Life* (New Haven, CT: Yale University Press, 2006), p. 61.

Chapter 5: The Second Republic

1. Gerhard Masur, *Simón Bolívar* (Albuquerque, NM: University of New Mexico Press, 1969), p. 114.

2. G.E. Fitzgerald (ed.), *The Political Thought of Bolivar: Selected Writings* (Netherlands: Springer, 1971), p. 18.

3. David Bushnell, *Simón Bolívar: Liberation and Disappointment* (New York, NY: Pearson Longman, 2004), p. 49.

4. Augusto Mijares, *The Liberator* (Caracas, Venezuela: North American Association of Venezuela, 1991), p. 240.

5. Guillermo Sherwell, "Simón Bolivar: The Liberator." Retrieved December 22, 2016. https://archive.org/stream/simonbolivarthel006967mbp/simonbolivarthel006967mbp_djvu.txt.

6. John Lynch, "Simón Bolívar and the Spanish American Revolutions," *History Today,* July 1983, p. 7.

7. James A. Woods and John Charles Chasteen, *Problems in Modern Latin American History: Sources and Interpretations* (New York, NY: Rowman & Littlefield, 2009), p. 7.

8. Simón Bolívar, "Reply of a South American to a Gentleman of this Island [Jamaica]," in Lewis Bertrand (trans), *Selected Writings of Bolivar.* (New York, NY: The Colonial Press, 1951). http://faculty.smu.edu/bakewell/BAKEWELL/texts/jamaica-letter.html.

9. Simón Bolívar in *Carta de Jamaica.* Gert Osstindie (ed.), *Ethnicity in the Caribbean: Essays in Honor of Harry Hoetink* (Netherlands: Amsterdam University Press, 2006).

10. Sibylle Fischer, "Bolívar in Haiti: Republicanism in the Revolutionary Atlantic," in Carla Calarge, *Haiti and the Americas.* (Jackson, MI: University Press of Mississippi, 2013), p. 38.

11. Mijares, p. 284.

12. Kathy Wilmore, "El Libertador: Simon Bolivar Led—and Won—the Struggle for South America's Independence, Becoming a Hero in Five Nations,. Junior Scholastic, March 21, 2005. https://www.thefreelibrary.com/El+libertador%3A+Simon+Bolivar+led--and+won--the+struggle+for+South...-a0130723440.

13. Simón Bolívar, "An Address of Bolivar at the Congress of Angostura (February 15, 1819)," University of Dayton. Retrieved December 22, 2016, http://homepages.udayton.edu/~santamjc/angosturatxt.html.

14. John Lynch, *Simón Bolívar: A Life* (New Haven, CT: Yale University Press, 2006), p. 29.

15. Richard W. Slatta and Jane Lucas De Grummond, p. 220.

16. Marie Arana, *Bolívar: American Liberator.* (New York, NY: Simon & Schuster, 2013), p. 284.

17. Simón Bolívar,AZ Quotes. Retrieved February 13, 2017. http://www.azquotes.com/quote/716676.

Chapter 6: Presidente Bolívar

1. Augusto Mijares, *The Liberator* (Caracas, Venezuela: North American Association of Venezuela, 1991), p. 333.

2. Mijares, p. 344.

3. John Lynch, *Simón Bolívar: A Life* (New Haven, CT: Yale University Press, 2006), p. 39.

4. Frederick H. Fornoff and David Bushnell, *El Libertador: Writings of Simón Bolívar* (New York, NY: Oxford University Press, 2003), p. 34.

5. Bolívar, "An Address of Bolivar at the Congress of Angostura (February 15, 1819)." University of Dayton. Retrieved December 22, 2016, http://homepages .udayton.edu/~santamjc/angosturatxt.html.

6. Fornoff and Bushnell, p. 34.

7. Mijares, p. 28.

8. Mijares, p. 50.

9. Mijares, p. 28.

10. John Lynch, "Simón Bolívar and the Spanish Revolutions," *History Today*, 1983. http://www .historytoday.com/john-lynch/simon-bolivar-and -spanish-revolutions.

11. Pamela S. Murray, *For Glory and Bolívar: The Remarkable Life of Manuela Sáenz* (Austin, TX: University of Texas Press, 2008), p. 54.

12. Murray, p. 30.

13. Gerhard Masur, "The Liberator is Immortal": An Unknown Letter of Manuela Sáenz," *Hispanic American Historical Review* 29(3), 1949, p. 381.

14. Mijares, , p. 419.

15. Lynch, p. 213.

16. Nancy Elena Ferreira Gomes, "Bolívar: 200 Years After," *International Relations* 2(1), p. 138.

17. Mijares, p. 2.

18. José Félix Díaz Bermúdez, "Bolívar and Democracy," *Americas* 62(5), 2010, p. 51.

19. Germán Carrera Damas, "The Hidden Legacy of Simón Bolívar," in David Bushnell and Lester D. Langley (Eds). *Simón Bolívar: Essays on the Life and Legacy of the Liberator* (New York, NY: Rowman & Littlefield Publishers, 2008), p. 166.

20. Mijares, p. 288.

21. Lynch, p. 276.

22. Mijares, p. 551.

Chapter 7: The Passing of El Libertador

1. John Lynch, *Simón Bolívar: A Life.* (New Haven: Yale University Press, 2006), p. 274.

2. Augusto Mijares, *The Liberator.* (Caracas: North American Association of Venezuela, 1991), p. 569.

3. Lynch, p. 276.

4. Mijares, p. 556.

5. Simón Bolívar, "Proclamation to the People of Colombia," in Gerald E. Fitzgerald (Ed.), *The Political Thought of Bolívar*, (Netherlands: Springer, 1971), pp. 136-137.

6. Mijares, p. 106.

7. Tom Phillips and Virginia Lopez, "Hugo Chávez Claims Simón Bolívar was Murdered not Backed by Science," *Guardian*, July 26, 2011. https://www.theguardian .com/world/2011/jul/26/hugo-chavez-liberation -hero- murdered.

8. Richard W. Slatta and Jane Lucas De Grummond, *Simón Bolívar's Quest for Glory.* (College Station, TX: Texas A&M University Press, 2003), p. 301.

Chapter 8: Bolívar's Legacy

1. Jennifer P. Baker, "The Gran Plan," *Calliope* 24(4), 2014, p. 24.

2. Villamarín Pulido, *The Delirium of the Liberator* (Bogotá, Colombia: Penclips Publicidad y Deseño, 2006), p. 7.

3. Gerhard Masur, *Simón Bolívar* (Albuquerque, NM: University of New Mexico Press, 1969), p. 399.

4. Sidney Lens, *The Forging of the American Empire: From the Revolution to Vietnam* (London: Pluto Press, 2003), p. 89.

5. Luis Marden, "Caracas, Cradle of the Liberator," *National Geographic* 77(4), 1940, p. 507.

6. "The Military Career of Hugo Chavez," In Depth Info, 2016. http://www.indepthinfo.com/hugo-chavez/military-career.htm.

7. Germán Carrera Damas, "The Hidden Legacy of Simón Bolívar," in Bushnell and Langley, p. 159.

8. John Lynch, *Simón Bolívar: A Life*. (New Haven: Yale University Press, 2006),, p. 9.

9. Janice Hammer, "Liberator," *Opera News* 59(8), 1995, p. 21.

10. UNESCO, "The International Simon Bolivar Prize." Retrieved December 22, 2016, http://portal.unesco.org/culture/en/ev.php-URL_ID=9431&URL_DO=DO_TOPIC&URL_SECTION=201.html.

11. John Lombardi, "Epilogue: History and Our Heroes--The Bolívar Legend," in Bushnell and Langley, p. 181.

12. Ishaan Tharoor, "Simón Bolívar: The Latin American Hero Many Americans Don't Know," *Time*, May 31, 2013. http://world.time.com/2013/05/31/simon-bolivar- the-latin- american-hero- many-americans-dont-know.

GLOSSARY

armistice A formal agreement to stop fighting.

caudillo A military or political leader in Latin America.

criollo A white person of Spanish descent born in the New World.

dictator A ruler who has total power over a country.

Enlightenment An intellectual movement that advanced ideas such as liberty, reason, and the separation of church and state.

exile Being expelled and barred from one's native country.

hacienda A large estate in Latin America.

independistas Those seeking independence from Spanish rule.

junta A military group.

llaneros A cavalry of indigenous herders.

manifesto A written declaration of strongly held beliefs.

mantuano Someone belonging to the Venezuelan aristocracy.

mestizo A person of mixed ancestry, usually indigenous and European.

mulato Someone of African and European ancestry.

pardo A free person with some African ancestry.

peninsulares Those born in Spain (Iberian Peninsula) and living in the New World.

republic A form of government where the people elect representatives and elect a president to head the government.

royalist Someone loyal to Spain.

tuberculosis A deadly bacterial infection that attacks the lungs.

viceroy An appointed leader, representing royal authority.

wet nurse A woman who breastfeeds and cares for children who are not her own.

zambo A person of mixed indigenous and African ancestry.

FURTHER READING

Books

Arana, Marie. *Bolivar: American Liberator.* New York, NY: Simon & Schuster, 2014.

Harvey, Robert. *Bolívar: The South American Liberator.* New York, NY: Skyhorse Publishing, 2011.

Shanahan, Maureen, and Ana Maria Reyes. *Simón Bolívar: Travels and Transformations of a Cultural Icon.* Gainesville, FL: University Press of Florida, 2016.

Sherwell, Guillermo A. *Simón Bolívar: The Liberator.* Rockville, MD: Wildside Press, 2013.

Zeuske, Michael. *Simón Bolívar: History and Myth.* Princeton, NJ: Markus Wiener Publishers, 2012.

Websites

Embassy of Venezuela: Simón Bolívar
www.embavenez-us.org/kids.venezuela/simon.bolivar.htm
The Embassy of Venezuela provides a biography of the Liberator's life.

Encyclopedia Britannica: Simón Bolívar
www.britannica.com/biography/Simon-Bolivar
This website offers a thorough summary of Bolívar's life in both military and politics.

Films

Bolívar: Path to Glory, 2015
This Venezuelan production recounts Bolívar's life and
  military campaigns.

The Liberator, 2014
This is another famous Venezuelan production about
  Bolívar's life.

INDEX